MUIR OF THE MOUNTAINS

MUIR OF THE

MOUNTAINS

WILLIAM O. DOUGLAS

ILLUSTRATIONS BY
Daniel San Souci

Sierra Club Books for Children
SAN FRANCISCO

The many quotations in this book were taken from the following works by John Muir: *The Mountains of California, My First Summer in the Sierra, Our National Parks, The Story of My Boyhood and Youth,* and *The Yosemite.*

In order to make the text more readable, the usual practice of inserting ellipses to represent omissions in the quotations has not been observed in most cases, and the original paragraphing has occasionally been altered. Muir's spelling and styling have been retained, however.

Library of Congress Cataloging-in-Publication Data

Douglas, William O. (William Orville), 1898–
    Muir of the mountains / by William O. Douglas ; illustrations by Daniel San Souci.
        p.   cm.
    Originally published: Boston : Houghton Mifflin, 1961.
    Includes index.
    Summary: A biography of John Muir revealing the events and ideas that shaped America's pioneer conservationist and founder of the Sierra Club.
    ISBN 0-87156-505-6
    1. Muir, John, 1838–1914 — Juvenile literature.   2. Conservationists — United States — Biography — Juvenile literature.   3. Naturalists — United States — Biography — Juvenile literature.   [1. Muir, John, 1838–1914. 2. Conservationists.   3. Naturalists.]   I. San Souci, Daniel, ill.   II. Title.
QH31.M9D6 1994
333.72'092 — dc20
[B]   93-13680

Book and jacket design by Abigail Johnston
Composition by Wilsted & Taylor

10   9   8   7   6   5   4   3   2   1

CONTENTS

SCOTLAND

JOHN MUIR was born in Scotland on April 21, 1838. The surname Muir was an apt one for him, for the word in Scottish dialect means moor, or an uncultivated stretch of wasteland. John Muir was from his youth to his old age a lover of the outdoors. The wildness of nature was his great passion.

"When I was a boy in Scotland," Muir wrote, "I was fond of everything that was wild, and all my life I've been growing fonder and fonder of wild places and wild creatures. Fortunately around my native town of Dunbar, by the stormy North Sea, there was no lack of wildness, though most of the land lay in smooth cultivation. My earliest recollections of the country were gained on short walks with my grandfather when I was perhaps not over three years old."

John had two brothers and four sisters. His father ran a store in Scotland, and the family lived upstairs above it. But it was not a successful business, and the family was poor. In those days, their breakfast was simple oatmeal porridge; lunch was usually broth and mutton; tea was warm water with a little milk and sugar in it; and supper was boiled potatoes. At most meals barley scone was served. It was at this age that John, as might be expected, acquired the habit of eating very little — a habit that was to stay with him all his life.

Dunbar, on the coast of Scotland, had good schools and Muir's memory of them was pleasant: "I was sent to school before I had completed my third year. The first schoolday was doubtless full of wonders, but I am not able to recall any of them. I remember the servant washing my face and getting soap in my eyes, and mother hanging a little green bag with my first book in it around my neck so I would not lose it, and its blowing back in the sea-wind like a flag. But before I was sent to school my grandfather, as I was told, had taught me my letters from shop signs across the street.

"With my school lessons father made me learn hymns and Bible verses. For learning 'Rock of Ages' he gave me a penny, and I thus became suddenly rich. Scotch boys are seldom spoiled with money."

When John was eight he was studying English, French, and Latin. Other courses included spelling, history, arithmetic, and geography. There was much homework at night, for the next day's lessons had to be committed to memory. In those days, the teaching methods were rough-and-ready. The Scottish teachers were very strict. If a student did not know his lesson, if he slipped even a wee bit in reciting from memory, the teacher whipped him. These whippings were administered frequently, no favors shown, which led Muir in later years to say that in his school days in Scotland "there was a close connection between the skin and the memory."

John and his brothers also got thrashed by their father for not getting home until after dark, for fighting with other boys, and so on. The thrashings always took place at night, except when their father was not home. If he came in too late, he would thrash the boys in the morning.

A boy who was transferred to a new school had to take on all comers before his "fighting rank" was established. John once said: "An exciting time came when at the age of seven or eight years I left the auld Davel Brae school for the grammar school. Of course I had a terrible lot of fighting to do, because a new scholar had to meet every one of his age who dared to challenge him, this being the common introduction to a new school."

They had a game played with whips. Two boys, each with a whip, would stand facing each other and thrash one another on the legs until one quit from the pain. A band of boys from one school would challenge a band from another school, and a free-for-all fight would follow. The boys, convinced they were all going to be soldiers, thought these fights would make them tough and durable. But neither the schools nor the parents approved. If John came home at night with a black eye, his father would whip him, and the next morning his teacher would do the same. But for all the thrashings, the fighting went on behind the scenes.

There was more, however, than school books and fighting to John's education in Scotland. By the time John was eleven he had learned about three-fourths of the Old Testament and all of the New Testament. He could indeed recite the New Testament from the beginning of Matthew to the end of Revelations, without stopping once.

There were also days when the boys escaped to the hills. John wrote: "To improve our speed and wind, we often took long runs into the country. A dozen or so of us would start out on races that were simply tests of endurance, running on and on along a public road over the breezy hills like hounds, without stopping or getting tired. The only serious trouble we ever felt in these long races was an occasional stitch in our sides. One of the boys started the story that sucking raw eggs was a sure cure for the stitches. We had hens in our back yard, and on the next Saturday we managed to swallow a couple of eggs apiece, a disgusting job, but we would do almost anything to mend our speed, and as soon as we could get away after taking the cure we set out on a ten- or twenty-mile run to prove its worth. We thought nothing of running right ahead ten or a dozen miles before turning back; for we knew nothing about taking time by the sun, and none of us had a watch in those days. Indeed, we never cared about time until it began to get dark. Then we thought of home and the thrashing that awaited us. Late or early, the thrashing was sure, unless father happened to be away.

"Oh, the blessed enchantment of those Saturday runaways in the prime of the spring! How our young wondering eyes reveled in the sunny, breezy glory of the hills and the sky, every particle of us thrilling and tingling with the bees and glad birds and glad streams! Kings may be blessed; we were glorious, we were free— school cares and scoldings, heart thrashings and flesh thrashings alike, were forgotten in the fullness of nature's glad wildness."

John and his friends took every chance to visit the fields and woods and explore the wildness of nature. These were John's first explorations of wilderness areas—the beginning of wanderings and research that lasted all his life.

One of his interests was in birds. He learned their names and their habits. He loved to collect bird nests—after the young brood had been hatched and left. He captured some young birds and tried to raise them in cages, but they never thrived and he always turned them loose. The skylarks of Scotland were his favorite, and he spent hours watching them soar into the sky until they were out of sight. He loved birds dearly all his life, and his heart was almost broken as a boy in Scotland when he saw a soldier rob a robin's nest and carry the young birds off to sell in the market. In the spring when the swallows returned to Scotland, he had a song he sang—"Welcome, welcome, little stranger."

John later wrote about his early interest in birds: "Our amusement on Saturday afternoons and vacations depended mostly on getting away from home into the country, especially in the spring when the birds were calling loudest. Father sternly forbade [my brother] David and me from playing truant in the fields with plundering wanderers like ourselves, fearing we might go on from bad to worse, get hurt in climbing over walls, caught by gamekeepers, or lost by falling over a cliff into the sea. 'Play as much as you like in the back yard and garden,' he said, 'and mind what you'll get when you forget and disobey.' Thus he warned us with an awfully stern countenance, looking very hard-hearted, while naturally his heart was far from hard, though he devoutly believed in eternal punishment for bad boys both here and hereafter. Nevertheless, like devout martyrs of wildness, we stole away to the sea-shore or the green, sunny fields with almost religious regularity, taking advantage of opportunities when father was very busy, to join our companions, oftenest to hear the birds sing and hunt their nests, glorying in the number we had discovered and called our own. A sample of our nest chatter was something like this: Willie Chisholm would proudly exclaim — 'I ken [know] seventeen nests, and you, Johnnie, ken only fifteen.'

"'But I wouldna gie my fifteen for your seventeen, for five of mine are larks and mavises. You ken only three o' the best singers.'

"'Yes, Johnnie, but I ken six goldies and you ken only one. Maist of yours are only sparrows and linties and robin-redbreasts.'

"Then perhaps Bob Richardson would loudly declare that he 'kenned mair nests than onybody,' for he kenned 'twenty-three, with about fifty eggs in them and mair than fifty young birds — maybe a hundred. Some of them naething but raw gorblings but lots of them as big as their mithers and ready to flee. And aboot fifty craw's nests and three fox dens.'

"'Oh, yes, Bob, but that's no fair, for naebody counts craws' nests and fox holes, and then you live in the country at Bellehaven where ye have the best chance.'"

The tides left big pools on the shore that John liked to explore. These pools contained queer creatures, including crawfish and eels. It was here he learned his love of water even before he could swim.

There was an old castle near Dunbar that was in great disrepair. John and his brother David used to climb over its highest walls and peaks. He said later in life that he took more chances on the walls of the old castle than any mountaineer would ever take.

John's bedroom had a dormer window, and after his mother had put them to bed, he and his brothers often crept out the window, crawled up the roof, and sat on top of it. The greatest difficulty was in getting down — a problem every mountaineer shares. Once his brother David lost courage and was marooned on the roof. They were afraid to call for help because they knew a whipping would be in store for them. John stood on the window sill, grabbed his brother securely by the feet, and held him that way while he slid off the roof. He dangled head down in the darkness until John, with an extra heave, hauled him feet first through the window. These escapades

in the old castle and on his father's rooftop were to stand him in good stead when years later he was climbing in the crags of Yosemite in California.

By the time John reached eleven, he had acquired certain habits that were to stay with him all his life. He spoke the Scottish dialect — *weel* for well, *gang* for go, *ken* for know, *maist* for most, *toon* for town, *hae* for have, *daur* for dare, *dae* for do, *alane* for alone, *greet* for cry, *skule* for school, *auld* for old, *bonnie* for good, and so on.

Though only Scottish was spoken out of school, pure English was taught in the classrooms. John spoke English with a perfect accent. He also learned in Scotland the knack of studying. He knew mental discipline and respected it. He also knew his Bible, and the early lessons stayed with him all his life. Lastly, he discovered some of the glories of nature in Scotland and loved all of them. That love for the wildness of the earth was to develop into a burning, enduring passion that soon dominated his life.

Then one night came exciting news. The Muirs were to leave Scotland and go to America. John's own words show the excitement of the occasion: "One night, when David and I were at grandfather's fireside solemnly learning our lessons as usual, my father came in with news, the most wonderful, most glorious, that wild boys ever heard. 'Bairns,' he said, 'you needna learn your lessons the nicht, for we're gan to America the morn!' No more grammar, but boundless woods full of mysterious good things; trees full of sugar, growing in ground full of gold; hawks, eagles, pigeons, filling the sky; millions of birds' nests, and no gamekeepers to stop us in all the wild, happy land. We were utterly, blindly glorious.

"After father left the room, grandfather gave David and me a gold coin apiece for a keepsake, and looked very serious, for he was about to be deserted in his lonely old age. And when we in fullness of young joy spoke of what we were going to do, of the wonderful birds and their nests that we should find, the sugar and gold, etc., and promised to send him a big box full of that tree sugar packed in gold from the glorious paradise over the sea, poor lonely grandfather, about to be forsaken, looked with downcast eyes on the floor and said in a low, trembling, troubled voice, 'Ah, poor laddies, poor laddies, you'll find something else ower the sea forbye gold and sugar, birds' nests and freedom fra lessons and schools. You'll find plenty hard, hard work.' And so we did."

They left right away, some of the family coming later. As John said: "Next morning we went by rail to Glasgow and thence joyfully sailed away from beloved Scotland, flying to our fortunes on the wings of the wings, carefree as thistle seeds. Father took with him only my sister Sarah (thirteen years of age), myself (eleven), and brother David (nine), leaving my eldest sister Margaret, and the three youngest of the family, Daniel, Mary, and Anna, with mother, to join us after a farm had been found in the wilderness and a comfortable house made to receive them."

FOUNTAIN
LAKE FARM

IT TOOK over six weeks for the Muirs to cross the Atlantic by ship, a journey we now take by air in a few hours. There were many immigrants aboard, and they had many discussions as to the places where they would settle in the New World. John later gave the following account of the decision made by his father during that journey: "My father started with the intention of going to the backwoods of Upper Canada. Before the end of the voyage, however, he was persuaded that the States offered superior advantages, especially Wisconsin and Michigan, where the land was said to be as good as in Canada and far more easily brought under cultivation; for in Canada the woods were so close and heavy that a man might wear out his life in getting a few acres cleared of trees and stumps. So he changed his mind and concluded to go to one of the Western States.

"On our wavering westward way a grain-dealer in Buffalo told father that most of the wheat he handled came from Wisconsin; and this influential information finally determined my father's choice. At Milwaukee a farmer who had come in from the country near Fort Winnebago with a load of wheat agreed to haul us and our formidable load of stuff to a little town called Kingston for thirty dollars. In leaving Scotland, father, like many other homeseekers, burdened himself with far too much luggage, as if all America were still a wilderness in which little or nothing could be bought. One of his big iron-bound boxes must have weighed about four hundred pounds, for it contained an old-fashioned beam-scales with a complete set of cast-iron counterweights, two of them fifty-six pounds each, a twenty-eight, and so on down to a single pound. Also a lot of iron wedges, carpenter's tools, and so forth, and at Buffalo, as if on the very edge of the wilderness, he gladly added to his burden a big cast-iron stove with pots and pans, provisions enough for a long siege, and a scythe and cumbersome cradle for cutting wheat, all of which he succeeded in landing in the primeval Wisconsin woods."

John's father located near Kingston, Wisconsin. He chose a quarter section that was blessed with a lake, and here the Muirs built a home, calling it Fountain Lake Farm. John described the building of this first house: "With the help of the nearest neighbors the little shanty was built in less than a day after the rough Bur Oak logs for the walls and the White Oak boards for the floor and roof were got together.

"To this charming hut, in the sunny woods, overlooking a flowery glacier meadow and a lake rimmed with white water-lilies, we were hauled by an ox-team across trackless carex swamps and low rolling hills sparsely dotted with round-headed Oaks. Just as we arrived at the shanty, before we had time to look at it or the scenery about it, David and I jumped down in a hurry off the load of household goods, for we had discovered a bluejay's nest, and in a minute or so we were up in the tree beside it, feasting our eyes on the beautiful green eggs and beautiful birds—our first memorable discovery. The handsome birds had not seen Scotch boys before and made a desperate screaming as if we were robbers like themselves; though we left the eggs untouched, feeling that we were already beginning to get rich, and wondering how many more nests we should find in the grand sunny woods. Then we ran along the brow of the hill that the shanty stood on, and down to the meadow, searching the trees and grass tufts and bushes, and soon discovered a bluebird's and a woodpecker's nest, and began an acquaintance with the frogs and snakes and turtles in the creeks and springs."

There was no schooling for the children; they all worked on the farm. John, being the oldest boy, had the greatest responsibility. At twelve years of age, he was so short that his head barely reached above the handles of the plow. But he became an excellent plowboy, and people said that no one could plow straighter than John.

He also helped clear the land. The trees had to be cut in the fields, and then the stumps had to be removed. It was John's job to chop them out. As many of them were two feet thick, it took a shovel and an axe to get at all the roots. That was hard work. John started

at 4:00 A.M. and worked until noon, when everyone took an hour out for "dinner." Then back to the fields John went—working until dark and having his supper about nine. Then he would sit with his father, mother, sisters, and brothers for prayer and Bible reading and finally get to bed about ten. The day was at least sixteen hours in the summer and about as long in the winter. All work was by hand—even the cutting and threshing of the wheat. The hours were much too long for a boy. John sometimes got sick, but even then his father sent him to the fields. Once when he had the mumps he almost fainted at his work, but his father kept him at it. Finally John came down with pneumonia and had to go to bed. He lay gasping for weeks, for there were no miracle drugs to cure him, no doctors nearby. But he pulled through, and back to the fields he went.

But there were also times when John and his brothers managed to go exploring in the Wisconsin woods. Whether hiking or working, John always kept looking for wildlife. Wisconsin in those days had not yet been plowed. What John found was a wilderness, not touched by civilization. He called it "pure wildness," and every lesson he learned from it he called "a love lesson"—a lesson about trees, grass, flowers, and animals.

It was here at Fountain Lake Farm that John got the idea that some land should never be changed or molested. There was one particular meadow that he thought should be preserved in its natural condition. Later he tried to buy this meadow and fence out all domestic animals. But he never succeeded in getting the owner to sell. This idea of preserving some land in its natural state grew in his mind until, years later, it developed into the idea of the national park—for which John Muir was to become famous.

His father continued his habit of thrashing the boys for misdeeds. Even when John had done nothing wrong, his father would thrash him at night, saying, "I dinna ken any wrong ye have done this day but I'll thrash ye the same for I hae no doubt ye deserve it." These whippings made John want to escape the house and spend his time outdoors. The lessons he learned in the woods were not whipped into him. The hours he spent there made up for his long hours of work and the demands of his father.

He loved the horses and the cows and his dog, Watch. He liked to hitch up an old sow when his father was not around and make her go in harness. This sow had a litter of pigs that she took to the woods looking for acorns. There were Indians in Wisconsin in those days, and one shot a baby pig. The old sow rushed back to the farm with her remaining little ones, all out of breath and terror-stricken. John never forgot the fear in her eyes—a look as penetrating as any in the eyes of a person. The terror he saw in the sow made him realize that beasts too have feelings, that there is a "oneness," as John put it, in people and all the other living things on earth.

Of all the wonders of nature that Wisconsin offered in those days, the most glorious for John were the birds. The chickadees and nuthatches stayed all year round, and John saw that they were fed during the long, severe Wisconsin winters. These were his favorites, for their cheery songs brightened the coldest weather. On winter nights he listened to the eerie music of the owls. The prairie chicken stayed all winter too, roosting in tall trees at night and feeding in the unhusked cornfields and on the buds of birch and willow.

The bluebirds were the first to arrive in the spring, and John soon learned their mating and nesting habits. He loved them especially for the way they would protect their young by attacking anyone who approached their nests. He admired the way the kingbird drove away hawks that tried to rob the nest. The brown thrushes had the same courage, chasing squirrels and snakes that came too near their young. The bobolinks, to John, sang more eloquently than any other bird. The redwing blackbirds too were gay singers, and after their nesting cares were over they assembled in flocks of hundreds of thousands to feast in the cornfields. Then they would gather in trees and sing like a congregation in church. The meadowlark, Baltimore oriole, scarlet tanager, and speckle-breasted song sparrow all became John's friends; he soon knew all their habits.

In the fall millions of ducks came by Fountain Lake looking for the wild rice that then grew in Wisconsin waters. Canada geese also were autumn visitors. John studied them and observed how cautious they were. They flew several times around a field before alighting in it, looking for possible enemies in thickets or other hiding places. While the flock fed, one gander always stood guard to sound the alarm. After a while, that gander would be relieved as another took his place, giving him a chance to eat. Once John caught a crippled goose that let out a piercing cry of terror. The leader of the flock heard the cry and wheeled in the air, circling back to where John stood with the crippled bird. The leader then dived at the boy, trying to save his wounded friend. This courage and spirit of the gander made John realize how bold and devoted the geese were.

After eight years of hard work, the Muirs had made Fountain Lake Farm an attractive place. They had cut the forests, cleared the fields, built fences, erected barns, and had a comfortable home. But John's father was not content. He bought 320 acres of wild land and began all over again to clear it and build a new house. Much more dreary chopping, digging, and plowing were necessary. By this time John was twenty and doing a man's work. He carried the main burden on this new farm, a place they called Hickory Hill because of a stand of hickory trees near the farmhouse, which they located on a height of land. But this farm had no good water. A well had to be dug, and that job was assigned to John. The first ten feet proved easy going; then John struck sandstone. His father tried blasting the rock, but that did not work. John had to dig the rock out with chisels and hammers. The hole was about three feet wide. John sat in it day after day from sunrise to dark. He chipped away for weeks on end. His father, or brother David, would lower a bucket to haul up the chips, and at noon and at night they would pull up John. One morning when the hole was eighty feet deep, John was lowered to the bottom and almost suffocated. Gas from carbonic acid had settled in the bottom of the well — the thing miners call choke-damp. Fortunately

John was able to shout to his father, who pulled him out. The gas made him terribly sick, so thereafter they threw water into the well to absorb the gas and dropped bundles of hay on a rope into the hole to stir up the gas and inject pure air. After months of working in this hole, John finally hit water at ninety feet.

STUDENT AND INVENTOR

THERE WAS no school for John, and in spite of his long working hours, he wanted to study. He persuaded his father to buy an arithmetic book. In one summer he mastered it, studying at noon after he had eaten and before he returned to the fields. Then he started on algebra, geometry, and trigonometry — acting as his own teacher just as Abraham Lincoln had done. He borrowed many books from neighbors, including Sir Walter Scott's novels, Plutarch's *Lives,* Shakespeare, Milton, and others.

Even after a full day in the fields, John liked to steal a few minutes to read before going to bed. Bedtime in the summer was ten o'clock, in the winter eight. His father had always punished the children if they sat up after these hours. John got his father to agree that if he went to bed promptly he could get up early to read. So in the winter John retired at eight and got up at one in the morning to read and study. It was cold those winter mornings. He knew his father would object if he made a fire with the wood they had worked so hard to cut, so he decided to build a sawmill.

He set up a workshop in the basement. He had a vise and a file, but no saw. Taking a strip of steel from a woman's corset and filing teeth in it, he made a fine-tooth saw that would handle hard wood. He dammed up a small stream, and the falling water turned a wheel that operated the saw. Now he could easily cut all the wood he needed.

John had never seen the inside of a clock or watch, and there was none in the family. He figured out in his own mind how a clock should be made. He constructed one from wood, whittling all the pieces in his spare time. His father learned of it and told him to stop making a clock and start studying the Bible. But John secretly continued with the project. He used rocks for weights that slowly pulled the chain that turned the wheels. When the clock was finished, he put it in the parlor of the farmhouse. It ran well, having a loud tick and striking on the hour. Although his father was greatly impressed, he said nothing.

John made other clocks. He also made a thermometer from an iron rod taken from an old wagon box. He discovered that the rod would expand when it was heated and contract when cold. He measured the contraction and expansion by a series of levers he made from strips of old hoop iron. The slightest change in the length of the rod was instantly shown on a dial. John placed the thermometer on the side of the house. It was so large it could be seen from the

fields. The thermometer was extremely sensitive, even to the heat of a person's body — when one stood four or five feet from it, the dial would move. This thermometer was the wonder of the countryside. Even John's father was pleased.

John was now twenty-two and eager to leave home. Having come of age, he was legally free to do as he pleased. A neighbor urged him to take his inventions to the State Fair at Madison, Wisconsin. So off he went, a few dollars in his pocket and a package over his shoulder. John wrote about it later: "When I told father that I was about to leave home, and inquired whether, if I should happen to be in need of money, he would send me a little he said, 'No; depend entirely on yourself.' Good advice, I suppose, but surely needlessly severe for a bashful, home-loving boy who had worked so hard. I had the gold sovereign that my grandfather had given me when I left Scotland, and a few dollars, perhaps ten, that I had made by raising a few bushels of grain on a little patch of sandy abandoned ground. So when I left home to try the world I had only about fifteen dollars in my pocket.

"Strange to say, father carefully taught us to consider ourselves very poor worms of the dust . . . and devoutly believed that quenching every spark of pride and self-confidence was a sacred duty, without realizing that in so doing he might at the same time be quenching everything else. Praise he considered most venomous, and tried to assure me that when I was fairly out in the wicked world making my own way I would soon learn that although I might have thought him a hard taskmaster at times, strangers were far harder.

On the contrary, I found no lack of kindness and sympathy. All the baggage I carried was a package made up of the two clocks and a small thermometer made of a piece of old washboard, all three tied together."

This was in September 1860, just before the Civil War. He was warmly greeted at the fair. He displayed his inventions in a booth, and they attracted more attention than any other exhibit. He received many notices in the newspapers and a prize of fifteen dollars.

John entered the University of Wisconsin (after spending a few weeks in a preparatory school) and worked his way throughout his school years. Later John wrote about those days: "During the . . . years that I was in the University, I earned enough in the harvest-fields during the long summer vacations to carry me through the balance of each year, working very hard, cutting with a cradle four acres of wheat a day, and helping to put it in the shock. But, having to buy books and paying, I think, thirty-two dollars a year for instruction, and occasionally buying acids and retorts, glass tubing, bell-glasses, flasks, etc., I had to cut down expenses for board now and then to half a dollar a week.

"One winter I taught school ten miles south of Madison, earning much-needed money at the rate of twenty dollars a month, 'boarding round,' and keeping up my University work studying at night."

The winter he taught school he had to start a fire in the school-house at 8:00 A.M. to get it warm for the students. He invented a way of doing this mechanically. He set up a wooden clock above the stove. He filled the stove with kindling and wood the night before and placed on top a teaspoonful of powdered chlorate of potash and sugar. Finally he fixed the clock so that at eight in the morning it would trip a lever and drop a bit of sulphuric acid on the powder. That started the fire. It worked every morning all winter long.

John made other inventions. He geared his clock to a collapsible bed. When the appointed hour came, the bed tipped up, dumping him on the floor. He manufactured these beds and sold a few to help pay his college expenses; boys bought them for the fun they caused. John went one step further, and to his amusement had the clock tip the bed and light a lamp at the same time. John invented a desk in which all his books were placed in the order in which his classes came. He hooked up this desk with the clock, which then dumped him on the floor, lit a lamp, and pushed the first book onto the desk. After a certain number of minutes, the clock would return that book to its stall and move up the next one.

In the summer John had the sun tip the bed that put him on the floor. He did this by fastening a magnifying glass to the sill of his bedroom window and focusing it so that the rays would burn a thread, causing the bed to collapse. He made so many inventions during his college days that his room became a showplace for visitors. His clock is still on exhibit at the Wisconsin State Historical Society.

John was considered a genius, principally because of his inventions — and perhaps in small part because of his rough homemade clothes and a beard that he left untrimmed.

After he left college, John went to Canada for a time. At Meaford, Ontario, he was employed by a company that manufactured handles for brooms and rakes. John improved the handle-making machine and made it more completely automatic, with the result that the factory's output of handles was nearly doubled. His machine turned out eight handles a minute, and the company was a great success, thanks to John's invention. But one night the factory caught fire and burned. The loss was total, and there was no insurance.

After the factory burned, John left Canada and went to Indianapolis to work for Osgood, Smith & Company, the largest manufacturer of carriage parts in the country. He was promoted rapidly because of his skill in improving the manufacturing processes. He was made foreman and promised a partnership, but a curious accident changed his career.

He was unlacing a belt that drove a shaft of a machine when the file he was using to pull out the stitches in the leather slipped and pierced his right eye. He temporarily lost the sight of that eye, and the other eye, out of sympathy, also became blind. John thought he was permanently sightless. He lay for days in total darkness, fearing the worst. Gradually his sight returned, and though the right eye was never perfect, it regained partial vision.

During the long weeks of blindness, John was plagued with painful thoughts. Never again would he ever see fields of flowers. Never again would he see the flight of birds and their radiant plumage. Sunsets and sunrises, whose beauties he loved, would be forever lost to him. He thought he had seen the last fingers of lightning in the sky, the last trees bowing before great gales, the last fleecy clouds racing across blue skies, the last blue waters lapping at the lake's edge. The darkness of the new world he had come to know would wipe out most of the glories of the outdoors he had come to love.

During the depressing hours of his suffering he decided that if his sight did return he would give all of his life to the outdoors. No more factories, no more workshops, no more machinery, no more lathes. He resolved that if he could see again, he would turn his face to the fields and the woods. His inventions had been interesting to him. More interesting were what he liked to call "the inventions of God." By these he meant the flowers, grasses, shrubs, lakes, woods, birds, animals, and mountains. The invention of God he loved the most was the wilderness and all its plants and animal life. In the long days of darkness when he fought the battle against blindness, the glories of the outdoors seemed to him to be the greatest of all. If he could ever see again he would make the woods and meadows his workshop. And that is exactly what he did. An accident in a carriage shop turned this man from inventions to the outdoors and gave to America a great conservationist in a time of need.

A LONG
EXCURSION

ALL HIS LIFE John had been interested in flowers, grasses, shrubs, and trees. When he entered the University of Wisconsin he studied them in earnest. In the summers, while he was doing farm work to earn money to pay his college expenses, he collected flowers and plants during the noon hour. He kept the plants fresh in water and at night classified them. By the end of the first year he knew the principal flowering plants of the Wisconsin area.

John's trips into the woods and fields in search of flowers continued even when he worked in the factories. Both in Canada and in Indiana, where he was nearly blinded, his off hours were spent in meadows and woods looking for old and new floral friends.

After his accident he returned to Wisconsin to visit his parents and friends, and there he decided to go south to see the vegetation of "the warm end of the country" and on to South America to study tropical flowers. He went by rail to Louisville, Kentucky, and from

28

that city he walked 1000 miles to Florida and the Gulf of Mexico. This hike started on September 1, 1867, and he reached Florida six or seven weeks later.

John went cross-country, avoiding as many cities as he could. He carried no bedroll. He had a small rubber bag that held a change of underclothes, comb, towel, soap, brush, and three books—the New Testament, *Paradise Lost* by Milton, and Burns's *Poems*. The only other thing he carried was a small wooden press for the plants he would collect. John put it this way: "When I set out on the long excursion that finally led to California, I wandered, afoot and alone, from Indiana to the Gulf of Mexico, with a plant-press on my back, holding a generally southward course, like the birds when they are going from summer to winter."

He had a small amount of money with him and usually arranged to have supper and breakfast with some farm family, paying for his board and bed. Many families—both white and black—took him in. But more often than not, there was no bed in the house for him, so he slept "with the trees in the one great bedroom of the open night." Many people at first suspected him of being a criminal, for in the days immediately following the Civil War, the South was filled with lawless men who wandered through the countryside, robbing and stealing. But John's frank and open face and direct way of speaking soon convinced everyone he was a man to trust.

Still, one of his problems was to avoid robbers and highwaymen. He had to cross two mountain ranges—the Cumberland and the

Blue Ridge—which in those days were filled with bandits. Usually these bandits took John to be an herb doctor. Herb doctors were fairly numerous in the mountains of the South, where they went about collecting leaves and roots from which they made medicines. Generally they were poor men, so when the bandits saw John with his plant press full of herbs and flowers, they did not bother him.

On October 8, 1867, he reached Savannah, Georgia, where he expected to find money sent by his brother. But there was none either at the express office or the post office. That night he spent at the cheapest lodginghouse he could find. No money arrived the next day. This left John with twenty-five cents. He looked for work and could find none. He therefore decided to ration his money, spending three cents a day for food—a sum that would buy only a few crackers or a little bread. He could not afford lodging, and there were so many thieves in the neighborhood he hesitated to sleep by the roadside or on the beach. He had a bright idea. People were ordinarily afraid of cemeteries at night, believing that spirits were abroad then, so John concluded he would be safe there.

The name of the cemetery was Bonaventure, and John found it to be one of the most interesting places he had ever seen. Live oaks lined the main driveway, their branches touching overhead. These trees were adorned with silvery gray moss eight or ten feet in length, and the effect of the moss-hung trees was glorious to John. He found many birds in the cemetery—bald eagles, crows, warblers, and others. Butterflies, toads, and snakes were there too, and John spent hours watching them. His days in these burial grounds made him think a lot about life and death, and after a week he concluded that death is a part of the divine harmony of life, that the two are inseparable.

John made a small bed under some bushes and a thick mattress of the long moss. He placed branches overhead so that they rested in forks of the bushes on each side and thatched it with rushes. Now he was protected from the dew.

Every day he went to town, hoping for the arrival of some money. Five days passed and he had only ten cents left. And he had eaten so little that he was becoming faint. As he walked into town, the ground seemed to be rising up in front of him, and the water in the ditches alongside the road seemed to be flowing uphill. He realized he was dangerously hungry. Good fortune was with him this day, for the money arrived. The first food he bought was fresh gingerbread, which a woman on the street was selling.

From Savannah — which is on the Atlantic Ocean — John went by boat to northern Florida and then walked across Florida to Cedar Keys on the Gulf — a town just about opposite Daytona Beach. In those days Georgia and Florida were infested with malaria-bearing mosquitoes. Somewhere along the line John had been bitten by an infected mosquito. In Cedar Keys he contracted malaria and was seriously ill.

He was nursed back to health by some kind people, and by January 1868 he was on his way. He described his next trip: "From the

west coast of Florida I crossed the Gulf to Cuba, enjoyed the rich tropical flora there for a few months, intending to go thence to the north end of South America, make my way through the woods to the head waters of the Amazon, and float down that grand river to the ocean. But I was unable to find a ship bound for South America—fortunately, perhaps, for I had incredibly little money for so long a trip and had not yet fully recovered from a fever caught in the Florida swamps."

Unable to find a vessel going south, he turned north, traveling by boat to New York City. He called New York a city of "terrible canyons." He did not like it at all. He had heard about California and the famous Yosemite Valley. So he found a ship sailing for San Francisco by way of Panama. Steerage passage was only forty dollars. John bought a ticket and sailed with many other emigrants for California. The boat landed in Panama. There was no Panama Canal then. John and the others went by train to the Pacific side of the isthmus and caught a boat sailing north.

He arrived in San Francisco on March 28, 1868, to open new and glorious chapters in his life. Yosemite with its wonderful flora was his promised land. It lay just over the horizon to the east from the city. Now that it was so near at hand he could hardly wait to see it. This wondrous wilderness of which he had heard was like a magnet. Its pull was so strong he could spend only a brief time in San Francisco. On the morning of April 1, 1868, he was off to the mountain valley that now was to claim his heart for the rest of his life.

SHEEPHERDER AND SAWMILL OPERATOR

JOHN HEADED EAST to Yosemite on foot, carrying only a blanket, flour, and tea. Spring had come to the lower valleys. The larks were singing, and John was filled with excitement at the prospect of seeing Yosemite. His own words best describe his mood: "It was the bloom-time of the year over the lowlands and coast ranges. I wandered enchanted in long, wavering curves, knowing by my pocket map that Yosemite Valley lay to the east and that I should surely find it."

He found everything in the foothills interesting. Even the air seemed different — fresh and inspiring. The foothills, dotted with oaks, were purplish in the distance. But close at hand they were white, purple, and yellow from a host of wildflowers in bloom. The California quail, with a tuft on its head, was new to him. So was the chaparral — and many of the mints, lilies, and penstemon that grow in California.

When he reached the first ridge and looked across to the Sierra Nevada, he viewed nearly 300 miles of peaks covered with snow, more glorious, he thought, than any wilderness he had seen. The valleys were now knee-deep in flowers — the purple ones highest, the yellow ones somewhat lower, and beneath them a thick moss with purple stems and purple cups. What he wrote about this scene shows the depth of his feeling: "Looking eastward from the summit of the Pacheco Pass one shining morning, a landscape was displayed that after all my wanderings still appears as the most beautiful I have ever beheld. At my feet lay the Great Central Valley of California, level and flowery, like a lake of pure sunshine, forty or fifty miles wide, five hundred miles long, one rich furred garden of yellow compositae. And from the eastern boundary of this vast golden flower-bed rose the mighty Sierra, miles in height, and so gloriously colored and so radiant, it seemed not clothed with light, but wholly composed of it, like the wall of some celestial city. Along the top and extending a good way down, was a rich pearl-gray belt of snow; below it a belt of blue and dark purple, marking the extension of the forests; and stretching along the base of the range a broad belt of rose-purple; all these colors, from the blue sky to the yellow valley smoothly blending as they do in a rainbow, making a wall of light ineffably fine. Then it seemed to me that the Sierra should be called, not the Nevada or Snowy Range, but the Range of Light."

At Coulterville — a small mining town — he bought more flour and tea. Hearing that the Sierra was filled with bears, and not

knowing that this animal seldom attacks people, John bought an old army gun. There was still snow in the mountains, but he kept climbing. As he went higher there were new and different forests—yellow pines, sugar pines, red firs, Douglas fir, and the great sequoias. Never had Muir seen any tree as big and magnificent as the sequoia.

He spent a month in the Sierra, walking, camping, and seeing the sights. The trip cost only three dollars. On returning to the valley, John worked for a while in the harvest fields. Then he broke horses, worked on a ferry across the Merced River, and sheared sheep. That winter he herded sheep in the hills. John called the sheep "hoofed locusts" for the damage they did in eating the soil cover down to the roots and causing erosion. Later he was to campaign against allowing sheep in the Sierra.

This first winter in the foothills was interesting because of the new plants and animals he discovered. Flowers came up with the first fall rains, and with the flowers came the ants, birds, and rabbits. His knowledge of western wildlife grew every day. He found the water ouzel (now called dipper) and came to admire and love it. This is a small, bluish gray bird that feeds on water insects. It wades the streams and pushes over rocks with its bill, looking for food. Muir had these glowing words to say about this bird: ". . . best of all is the water-ouzel, a dainty, dusky little bird about the size of a robin, that sings a sweet fluty song all winter and all summer, in storms and calms, sunshine and shadow, haunting the rapids and waterfalls with marvelous constancy, building his nest in the cleft of a rock bathed in spray. He is not web-footed, yet he dives fearlessly into foaming rapids, seeming to take the greater delight the more boisterous the stream, always as cheerful and calm as any linnet in a grove. All his gestures as he flits about amid the loud uproar of the falls bespeak the utmost simplicity and confidence—bird and stream one and inseparable. What a pair! Yet they are well related. A finer bloom than the foam bell in an eddying pool is this little bird. We may miss the meaning of the loud-resounding torrent, but the flute-like voice of the bird—only love is in it."

John also learned how the golden eagle strikes down a rabbit with its "elbow" and then wheels, picks up the stunned animal with its claws, and goes to some high point to enjoy the feast.

By summer John was tired of the foothills. He wanted to go high into the Sierra. By chance he met a man who had over 2000 sheep and a sheepherder who was taking the flock into the high mountains. The owner hired John to go along to keep watch on the sheepherder and to help him when necessary. John described this new venture: "In the great Central Valley of California there are only two seasons—spring and summer. The spring begins with the first rainstorm, which usually falls in November. In a few months the wonderful flowery vegetation is in full bloom, and by the end of May it is dead and dry and crisp, as if every plant had been roasted in an oven.

"Then the lolling, panting flocks and herds are driven to the high, cool, green pastures of the Sierra. I was longing for the mountains about this time, but money was scarce. Mr. Delaney, a sheep-owner, for whom I had worked a few weeks, called on me, and offered to engage me to go with his shepherd and flock to the head-waters of the Merced and Tuolumne Rivers — the very region I had most in mind.

"I was fortunate in getting a fine St. Bernard dog for a companion. His master, a hunter with whom I was slightly acquainted, came to me as soon as he heard that I was going to spend the summer in the Sierra and begged me to take his favorite dog, Carlo, with me, for he feared that if he were compelled to stay all summer on the plains the fierce heat might be the death of him. 'I think I can trust you to be kind to him,' he said, 'and I am sure he will be good to you. He knows all about the mountain animals, will guard the camp, assist in managing the sheep, and in every way be found able and faithful.' Carlo knew we were talking about him, watched our faces, and listened so attentively that I fancied he understood us. Calling him by name, I asked him if he was willing to go with me. He looked me in the face with eyes expressing wonderful intelligence, then turned to his master, and after permission was given by a wave of the hand toward me and a farewell patting caress, he quietly followed me as if he perfectly understood all that had been said and had known me always."

And so on June 3, 1869, his sheep-camp outfit was on its way. In five days they reached the high mountains, John describing as follows his first night's sleep under the stars: "How deep our sleep last night in the mountain's heart, beneath the trees and stars, hushed by solemn-sounding waterfalls and many small soothing voices in sweet accord whispering peace! And our first pure mountain day, warm, calm, cloudless — how immeasurable it seems, how serenely wild! I can scarcely remember its beginning. Along the river, over the hills, in the ground, in the sky, spring work is going on with joyful enthusiasm, new life, new beauty, unfolding, unrolling in glorious exuberant extravagance — new birds in their nests, new winged creatures in the air, and new leaves, new flowers . . . rejoicing everywhere."

The early sheep camps were primitive, and the food came down mostly to beans and bread: "In the warm, hospitable Sierra, shepherds and mountain men in general, as far as I have seen, are easily satisfied as to food supplies and bedding. Most of them are heartily content to 'rough it,' ignoring Nature's fineness as bothersome or unmanly. The shepherd's bed is often only the bare ground and a pair of blankets, with a stone, a piece of wood, or a pack-saddle for a pillow. In choosing the spot, he shows less care than the dogs. His food, too, even when he has all he wants, is usually far from delicate, either in kind or cooking. Beans, bread of any sort, bacon, mutton, dried peaches, and sometimes potatoes and onions, make up his bill-of-fare. No two cooks quite agree on the methods of making beans do their best, and after petting and coaxing and nursing the savory mess — well oiled and mellowed with bacon boiled into the heart of it — the proud cook will ask, after dishing out a quart or two for trial, 'Well, how do you like *my* beans?' as if by no possibility could they be like any other beans cooked in the same way, but must needs possess some special virtue of which he alone is master. Molasses, sugar, or pepper may be used to give desired flavors; or the first water may be poured off and a spoonful or two of ashes or soda added to dissolve or soften the skins more fully, according to various tastes and notions. But, like casks of wine, no two potfuls are exactly alike to every palate."

This easy job with the sheepherder left many hours when John could climb and explore the high country in the Yosemite area. John wrote: "[I] followed the Mono Trail up the eastern rim of the basin nearly to its summit, then turned off southward to a small shallow valley that extends to the edge of the Yosemite.

"Following the ridge which made a gradual descent to the south, I came at length to the brow of that massive cliff that stands between Indian Cañon and Yosemite Falls, and here the far-famed valley came suddenly into view throughout almost its whole extent.

"I rambled along the valley rim to the westward; most of it is rounded off on the very brink, so that it is not easy to find places where one may look clear down the face of the wall to the bottom. When such places were found, and I had cautiously set my feet and drawn my body erect, I could not help fearing a little that the rock might split off and let me down, and what a down!—more than three thousand feet. Still my limbs did not tremble, nor did I feel the least uncertainty as to the reliance to be placed on them. My only fear was that a flake of the granite, which in some places showed joints more or less open and running parallel with the face of the cliff, might give way. After withdrawing from such places, excited with the view I had got, I would say to myself, 'Now don't go out on the verge again.' But in the face of Yosemite scenery cautious re-monstrance is vain; under its spell one's body seems to go where it likes with a will over which we seem to have scarce any control."

Muir loved to sketch in black and white, and he spent many hours on high peaks and ridges, drawing the startling views that lay in the distance or at his feet. One day he and his dog left camp for a day of sketching when he met his first bear. Bears had raided the sheep and killed a few, but Muir had never seen one. This morning he met one in a way that left a deep imprint in his mind: "I had not gone more than half a mile from camp this morning, when Carlo, who was trotting on a few yards ahead of me, came to a sudden, cau-tious standstill. Down went tail and ears, and forward went his knowing nose, while he seemed to be saying 'Ha, what's this? A bear, I guess.' Carlo came behind me, evidently sure that the bear was very near. So I crept to a low ridge of moraine boulders on the edge of a narrow garden meadow, and in this meadow I felt pretty sure the bear must be. I was anxious to get a good look at the sturdy mountaineer without alarming him; so drawing myself up noise-lessly back of one of the largest of the trees I peered past its bulging buttresses, exposing only a part of my head, and there stood neigh-bor Bruin within a stone's throw, his hips covered by tall grass and flowers, and his front feet on the trunk of a Fir that had fallen out into the meadow, which raised his head so high that he seemed to be standing erect. He had not yet seen me, but was looking and listening attentively, showing that in some way he was aware of our approach. I watched his gestures and tried to make the most of my opportunity to learn what I could about him, fearing he would catch sight of me and run away. For I had been told that this sort of bear, the cinnamon, always ran from his bad brother man, never showing fight unless wounded or in defense of young. He made a telling picture standing alert in the sunny forest garden. How well he played his part, harmonizing in bulk and color and shaggy hair with the trunks of the trees and lush vegetation, as natural a feature as any other in the landscape.

"After examining at leisure, noting the sharp muzzle thrust inquiringly forward, the long shaggy hair on his broad chest, the stiff erect ears nearly buried in hair, and the slow heavy way he moved his head, I thought I should like to see his gait in running, so I made a sudden rush at him, shouting and swinging my hat to frighten him, expecting to see him make haste to get away. But to my dismay he did not run or show any sign of running. On the contrary, he stood his ground ready to fight and defend himself, lowered his head, thrust it forward, and looked sharply and fiercely at me. Then I suddenly began to fear that upon me would fall the work of running; but I was afraid to run, and therefore, like the bear, held my ground. We stood staring at each other in solemn silence within a dozen yards or thereabouts, while I fervently hoped that the power of the human eye over wild beasts would prove as great as it is said to be. How long our awfully strenuous interview lasted, I don't know; but at length in the slow fullness of time he pulled his huge paws down off the log, and with magnificent deliberation turned and walked leisurely up the meadow, stopping frequently to look back over his shoulder to see whether I was pursuing him, then moving on again, evidently neither fearing me very much nor trusting me. He was probably about five hundred pounds in weight, a broad rusty bundle of ungovernable wildness, a happy fellow whose lines have fallen in pleasant places."

John spent six weeks with the herd of sheep and made many new discoveries—lilies so large that they would make bonnets for babies, red firs that were 240 feet high, and the dwarf white pine that grows at timberline and under whose low sprawling branches John often found a bed for himself. He found the bluebottle fly and bumblebee high in the Sierra, and the Douglas squirrel and the grasshopper too. And he loved them all. Thereafter he was never truly happy unless he was in the high mountains.

After doing odd jobs in the valley that fall, John decided to spend the winter in Yosemite. A few other men had preceded him. One was J. M. Hutchings, who had a home in Yosemite. John boarded with him. Hutchings wanted to saw the pines fallen in a windstorm and build cottages with the lumber. John agreed to help on the project. Using his skill as an inventor, he built a sawmill run by water power. With some of the first lumber John built himself a cabin. He dug a ditch to a creek and ran a stream through his cabin, so that he would have the music of the flowing water all night long. Soon ferns came up through the floorboards. Tree frogs came to live in the ferns, and common frogs were attracted by the water. He suspended his bed from the rafters and was sung to sleep not only by the water but by the music of the frogs as well.

Later he lived in the sawmill. He built a big box under the gables at one end of the mill and made it his home. He put two skylights in the roof—one so that he could see the peak called South Dome and the other so that he had a view of the upper Yosemite Falls. The window in the end gave him a full view of Yosemite Valley.

At night he read many books on plants and animals and the evolutions of life on this earth. At night he also classified the specimens of flowers he had collected on his hikes and gradually extended his knowledge of the wilderness. He expanded his interest to butterflies, made collections of them, and discovered a new species that was named for him.

During the two years he ran his sawmill he made many climbs into the Sierra, even in the wintertime. And of all the glories that he saw on these trips there were two that headed the list. The snowstorms greatly interested him. He came to know a snowflake as a composite of tiny six-rayed crystals that he called a snowflower. He liked to examine them, walking waist-deep in snow when the temperature was 12° F.

He came to know what snow banners are. A strong north wind whips and pounds snow crystals into snow dust. Some of the snow dust forms streamers that seem attached to the mountain peaks. They are a mile or more long and over 1000 feet wide. They appear to be silky, silvery banners. They are caused by the north wind sweeping up the bowl-like valleys of the Sierra and shooting the snow dust straight up to the peaks, where it is carried away horizontally. Muir saw them in great glory and in large numbers: "The most magnificent storm phenomenon I ever saw, surpassing in showy grandeur the most imposing effects of clouds, floods, or avalanches, was the peaks of the High Sierra, back of Yosemite Valley, decorated with snow-banners.

"I have seen only one display of this kind that seemed in every way perfect. This was in the winter of 1873, when the snow-laden summits were swept by a wild 'norther.' I happened at the time to be wintering in Yosemite Valley, that sublime Sierra temple where every day one may see the grandest sights. Yet even here the wild gala-day of the north wind seemed surpassingly glorious. I was awakened in the morning by the rocking of my cabin and the beating of pine-burs on the roof. Detached torrents and avalanches from the main windflood overhead were rushing wildly down the narrow side cañons, and over the precipitous walls, with loud resounding roar, rousing the Pines to enthusiastic action, and making the whole valley vibrate as though it were an instrument being played.

"But afar on the lofty exposed peaks of the range standing so high in the sky, the storm was expressing itself in still grander characters, which I was soon to see in all their glory. Innumerable peaks, black and sharp, rose grandly into the dark blue sky, their bases set in solid white, their sides streaked and splashed with snow, like ocean rocks with foam; and from every summit, all free and unconfused, was streaming a beautiful silky silvery banner, from half a mile to a mile in length, slender at the point of attachment, then widening gradually as it extended from the peak until it was about 1000 or 1500 feet in breadth, as near as I could estimate. The cluster of peaks called the 'Crown of the Sierra,' at the head of the Merced and Tuolumne Rivers — Mounts Dana, Gibbs, Conness, Lyell, Maclure, Ritter, with their nameless compeers — each had its own refulgent banner, waving with a clearly visible motion in the sun-glow, and there was not a single cloud in the sky to mar their simple grandeur."

Snow and frost and ice were to play important roles in the life of John Muir. For he was to learn that glaciers helped form the mountains and helped shape Yosemite and that they also ground up rocks so that the mosses, flowers, and trees would have soil for growth.

GLACIERS

JOHN MUIR had not been in the Sierra very long before he discovered the glaciers. Others had seen them and called them snowfields. Muir learned that some of these "snowfields," twenty or thirty feet down, were composed of blue ice, and that they were moving down the high valleys, pushing dirt and rock ahead of them.

A moraine is a ridge of dirt and rocks piled at the foot of a glacier. Muir found these in the Sierra, sixty to a hundred feet high, and above them tongues of snow and ice. There were deep cracks in these glaciers and Muir climbed down into them. Ice was melting and water was running far beneath, and when the water emerged at the end of the glacier it carried with it glacial silt, or "milk"—gray mud so fine and smooth it felt as though it had been powdered by a grindstone.

A glacier is, indeed, a grindstone. And Muir undertook at once to prove it. He drove stakes across one glacier in a straight line and

forty-six days later discovered that all of the stakes had moved down-hill, one of them moving forty-seven inches. He stretched a fishline across another glacier, tying the ends solidly on the banks. He drove a stake into the hard snow right beneath the fishline. He found that the stick was carried downhill about three-sixteenths of an inch a day.

This seemed to be proof enough that there were living glaciers in the Sierra. But some geologists did not believe it, and ten years after Muir's discovery one leading geologist, named Josiah Dwight Whitney, denied it.

Whitney had an even more serious dispute with Muir. Whitney advanced the theory that the deep valleys of the Sierra had been formed when the bottom had dropped out of the mountains in some ancient earthquake. Muir maintained that great glaciers once covered these ranges, dug out the valleys, and polished the rocks as they moved over them. Whitney's theory, however, was the one that people accepted. And when on March 26, 1872, the violent Inyo earthquake struck Yosemite, the white settlers as well as the Indians were terrified, convinced that the bottom was going to fall out of Yo-semite again. Many of them fled, but Muir stayed to see the sights. He had been sure that earthquakes had caused the rockslides that mark many of the slopes in the Sierra. And his theory was con-firmed by what he saw on the morning of March 26.

Muir wrote: "In Yosemite Valley, one morning about two o'clock, I was aroused by an earthquake; and though I had never before enjoyed a storm of this sort, the strange, wild thrilling motion and rumbling could not be mistaken, and I ran out of my cabin, near the Sentinel Rock, both glad and frightened, shouting, 'A noble earthquake!' feeling sure I was going to learn something. The shocks were so violent and varied, and succeeded one another so closely, one had to balance in walking as if on the deck of a ship among the waves, and it seemed impossible the high cliffs should escape being shattered. It was a calm moonlight night, and no sound was heard for the first minute or two save a low muffled underground rumbling and a slight rustling of the agitated trees, as if, in wrestling with the mountains, Nature were holding her breath. Then, suddenly, out of the strange silence and strange motion there came a tremendous roar. The Eagle Rock, a short distance up the valley, had given way, and I saw it falling in thousands of the great boulders I had been studying so long, pouring to the valley floor in a free curve luminous from friction, making a terribly sublime and beautiful spectacle—an arc of fire fifteen hundred feet span, as true in form and as steady as a rainbow, in the midst of the stupendous roaring rockstorm."

When Muir went up to examine the rock slide, the air was filled with the odor of crushed firs. The huge slide had indeed wiped out a forest of trees and smashed them as though they were weeds.

Muir wrote: "Shortly after sunrise, a low blunt muffled rumbling, like distant thunder, was followed by another series of shocks, which, though not nearly so severe as the first, made the cliffs and domes tremble like jelly, and the big Pines and Oaks thrill and swish and wave their branches with startling effect. The rocks trembled more or less every day for over two months, and I kept a bucket of water on my table to learn what I could of the movements. Nature, usually so deliberate in her operations, then created, as we have seen, a new set of features, simply by giving the mountains a shake — changing not only the high peaks and cliffs, but the streams. As soon as these rock avalanches fell every stream began to sing new songs; for in many places thousands of boulders were hurled into their channels, roughening and half damming them, compelling the waters to surge and roar in rapids where before they were gliding smoothly. Some of the streams were completely dammed, driftwood, leaves, etc., filling the interstices between the boulders, thus giving rise to lakes and level reaches."

Though these earthquakes did not cause the bottoms of the valleys to drop, the notion persisted that this had been the ancient cause of the formation of the Sierra canyons, and Whitney's case was apparently strengthened. Therefore Muir set out to make a detailed study of how glaciers could carve out valleys and submitted a public report on the matter.

The rock of the Sierra is very ancient — so many millions of years old that we can hardly imagine that length of time. The rock was once in an ocean that covered most of our West. Sediments were deposited underwater, forming layers of mud and gravel. Then pressures deep within the earth pushed these sediments up, cracked them, tilted them, folded them, and made them into mountain ranges. A long, long time later came molten granite, which tried to push up through the older rock. This fluid granite never broke through to the surface but remained at great depths, taking several million years to cool and solidify. A period of perhaps 40 million years followed when rains and wind eroded away the surface rock, uncovering the underlying granite. Then a long piece of the earth's crust, over 400 miles in length and about 70 miles in width, was gradually pushed upward along its eastern margin so as to tilt to the west and form the great uplift that we see today.

Following this came the Ice Age, which extended for perhaps a million years, when the glaciers grew, melted back, and then grew again. These glaciers, at their largest size, filled the Sierra canyons with ice thousands of feet thick. The ice was so thick it often spilled over one ridge down into another valley. Over a long period of time the glaciers receded as the climate got warmer. The great glaciers of the Ice Age probably disappeared as recently as 12,000 years ago. The ones John Muir saw and the ones we see today are only tiny remnants of the ancient ones.

Muir learned about the work of glaciers, not from books, but from the rocks, cliffs, ridges, and domes of the Sierra.

A tongue of thick ice passing over rock is like a carpenter's tool passing over wood. The direction of the flow of the ice can be determined by the markings left on the rocks. Ice is not a rigid solid but more like a very thick fluid. If it comes down one ridge, the downhill movement can push it up another ridge and down the far side. Muir traced the flow of ice over some ridges of the Sierra. He estimated the amount of digging and polishing these glaciers accomplished by studying the nature of the rock over which they moved.

The Sierra granite is usually not one solid mass. It is made up of bricklike blocks. Some of them stand almost erect. Others lie flat. Others produce domelike effects. Muir showed that as the glaciers moved over these mountains they made polished domes where the form of rock structure was strongest. The glaciers ripped apart bricklike blocks of granite that stood erect. They dug out thousands of tons of granite made up of bricklike horizontal blocks. These rocks, broken off by the glaciers, were in part ground up by the ice into fine powder and in part carried ahead of the glacier and deposited as moraines. Muir showed how the water collected above these moraines after the ice left and formed glacial lakes.

Muir's studies on glaciation in the Sierra were printed and distributed. They were lengthy and quite technical. Many thought they were ridiculous. One of those who still said they were unreliable was the famous geologist Josiah Dwight Whitney.

But time showed Muir to be essentially correct. Modern geologists can point out errors in his studies. But the report by the United States Geological Survey published in 1930 — sixteen years after Muir's death — recognized that Muir was right in maintaining that the glaciers had done much of the excavating in the Sierra. Later studies show that prior to the glaciers, the valleys of the Sierra had been V-shaped. After the glaciers they were U-shaped. Muir did not know all these things because he did not have the benefit of the deep borings that were subsequently made. All he knew he learned from the surface. This made his glacial studies the more remarkable. On the centennial of his birth a famous geologist paid Muir a fine tribute: "Muir was probably as nearly right in his glacial theory of the Yosemite as any scientist in the early seventies could have been."

STICKEEN

In order to broaden his studies of glaciation, John Muir went north to Alaska. In Muir's day most Yosemite glaciers had disappeared, but many in Alaska were active. Glaciers many miles long, several miles wide, and thousands of feet thick grind their way down from icy summits to the ocean's edge even now. By observing Alaskan glaciers at work, Muir could test his theories about the formation of the valleys and peaks of the Sierra.

He and his companions left Fort Wrangell in southeastern Alaska in canoes. One member of the party had a tiny black dog — a nondescript animal, a crossbreed of many species. It was so small and apparently helpless that Muir wanted to leave it behind. But the owner insisted that even though the dog was short-legged, rather houndish, and shaggy, it was very intelligent and very sturdy. He said the dog could endure cold like a bear and could swim like a seal. Its name was Stickeen, so called because of a tribe of Indians by that name.

Stickeen turned out to be a fine companion. In the many weeks when the party traveled by canoe, the dog always seemed to know what was going on. Though it slept most of the time, it woke up and paid sharp attention when seals or ducks appeared. It was smart enough to know from Muir's talk when the party was about to land. As the canoes headed in, the little dog would jump overboard and swim to the shore. Once on land it would disappear into the woods in search of squirrels and birds. When the canoes were ready to leave, the little dog could never be found. But Muir discovered that while he might not see the dog, the animal (hidden in the brush) was watching him. It always waited until the canoes were in deep water. Then it would dive into the surf and swim out to the canoes. Muir would lift the dog out of the ocean when it came alongside, hold it at arm's length for a moment to let the water run off, and then place it tenderly in the canoe.

These episodes happened over and over again. John Muir came to love Stickeen. And Stickeen became attached to Muir, following him wherever he went, no matter how thick the underbrush. Yet, as inseparable as Muir and the dog were, Stickeen never begged to be petted or scratched. He seemed to want to be left alone, seldom wagging his tail, seldom nuzzling Muir for affection. And he did not race or bark as most dogs do.

One day the party camped at Taylor Bay, in a spruce grove near a huge glacier that had recently moved down the slopes, uprooting great trees. Muir learned from the local Indians that this glacier moved about a mile a year, coming so far down into the river as to ruin their fishing.

Muir decided to explore the glacier the next day. He woke early and, while his companions and Stickeen were fast asleep, slipped out of camp without breakfast, putting a piece of bread in his pocket to eat later. It was a stormy, rainy day, the wind blowing a gale. Muir had not gone far before Stickeen came bouncing after him and would not go back, though Muir talked to him sternly. So off the two went together on what Muir later called the most memorable of his wild days.

They skirted the glacier for several miles, keeping within the edge of the woods. Then Muir with his axe chopped steps up the side of the mountain for himself and Stickeen. Once on top, Muir could not see to the other side, so wide was the icefield. Since the storm had abated a bit, he decided to walk across the glacier. The going was easy at first. Soon, however, they came to crevasses in the ice where Muir could look down a thousand feet or so. Some of these were twenty to thirty feet wide. Muir circled these. Others were two feet, six feet, or eight feet wide—and a thousand feet deep. Muir, using great care, jumped over them. And little Stickeen did the same, never hesitating a second, leaping through the air as though he were jumping a narrow ditch.

Muir had great admiration for the dog's performance: "The little adventurer was only about two years old, yet nothing seemed
novel to him, nothing daunted him. He showed neither caution nor
curiosity, wonder nor fear, but bravely trotted on as if glaciers were
playgrounds. His stout, muffled body seemed all one skipping mus-
cle, and it was truly wonderful to see how swiftly and to all appear-
ance heedlessly he flashed across nerve-trying chasms six or eight
feet wide. His courage was so unwavering that it seemed to be due
to dullness of perception, as if he were only blindly bold; and I kept
warning him to be careful. For we had been close companions on so
many wilderness trips that I had formed the habit of talking to him
as if he were a boy and understood every word."

It was seven miles across the icefield, and it took Muir and
Stickeen three hours to make it. Then they went up the glacier, exploring its branches. They spent so much time up there that when
they returned to the main glacier the day was pretty well gone. For
the first two miles of their return trip they had no trouble. Then
they reached a network of crevasses that slowed them down. They
searched for a narrow spot they could jump. Sometimes they walked
a mile to find such a passage. The sun was low, and to make matters
worse it started to snow. Now the cracks in the ice got wider. It was
all that Muir could do to jump them. He worried for himself and for
Stickeen too. If either of them missed by even the width of a hair, he
would die in an ice cave hundreds of feet deep. Muir had many close

calls in jumping these crevasses. But little Stickeen came hurtling over each, without any fear in his heart.

The farther toward camp they went, the deeper and wider became the crevasses—for they were returning by a different route than the one they had used that morning. Not much daylight was left when Muir came to a crevasse that was about twelve feet wide.

Muir wrote the following about this formidable cavern in the ice: "... the width of this jump was the utmost I dared attempt, while the danger of slipping on the farther side was so great that I was loath to try it. Furthermore, the side I was on was about a foot higher than the other, and even with this advantage the crevasse seemed dangerously wide. One is liable to underestimate the width of crevasses where the magnitudes in general are great. I therefore stared at this one mighty keenly, estimating its width and the shape of the edge on the farther side, until I thought that I could jump it if necessary, but that in case I should be compelled to jump back from the lower side I might fail. Now, a cautious mountaineer seldom takes a step on unknown ground which seems at all dangerous that he cannot retrace in case he should be stopped by unseen obstacles ahead. This is the rule of mountaineers who live long, and, though in haste, I compelled myself to sit down and calmly deliberate before I broke it.

"Should I risk this dangerous jump, or try to regain the woods on the west shore, make a fire, and have only hunger to endure while waiting for a new day? I had already crossed so broad a stretch of dangerous ice that I saw it would be difficult to get back to the woods through the storm, before dark, and the attempt would most likely result in a dismal night-dance on the the glacier; while just beyond the present barrier the surface seemed more promising, and the east shore was now perhaps about as near as the west. I was therefore eager to go on. But this wide jump was a dreadful obstacle."

At last Muir jumped and made it—but without any space to spare. Stickeen, however, hurtled across as though the space were a little ditch. In a few moments Muir came to a crevasse about fifty feet across—much too wide to jump. He went uphill almost a mile only to discover that the crack got wider. He went downhill and found the same condition. The only way across was by a narrow bridge of ice. Each end of the ice bridge was eight feet or more below the surface of the glacier. It drooped in the middle so that at its lowest point it was about thirty feet from the surface of the glacier.

Muir described how he planned this crossing: "Beginning, not immediately above the sunken end of the bridge, but a little to one side, I cut a deep hollow on the brink for my knees to rest in. Then, leaning over, with my short-handled axe I cut a step sixteen or eighteen inches below, which on account of the sheerness of the wall was necessarily shallow. That step, however, was well made; its floor sloped slightly inward and formed a good hold for my heels. Then, slipping cautiously upon it, and crouching as low as possible, with my left hand in a slight notch, while with the right I cut other similar steps and notches in succession, guarding against losing balance by glinting of the axe, or by wind-gusts, for life and death were in every stroke and in the niceness of finish of every foothold.

"After the end of the bridge was reached I chipped it down until I had made a level platform six or eight inches wide, and it was a trying thing to poise on this little slippery platform while bending over to get safely astride of the sliver. Crossing was then comparatively easy by chipping off the sharp edge with short, careful strokes, and hitching forward an inch or two at a time, keeping my balance with my knees pressed against the sides. The tremendous abyss on either hand I studiously ignored. To me the edge of that blue sliver was then all the world. But the most trying part of the adventure, after working my way across inch by inch and chipping another small platform, was to rise from the safe position astride and to cut a step-ladder in the nearly vertical face of the wall — chipping, climbing, holding on with feet and fingers in mere notches. At such times one's whole body is eye, and common skill and fortitude are replaced by power beyond our call or knowledge. Never before had I been so long under deadly strain. How I got up that cliff I never could tell. The thing seemed to have been done by somebody else."

Now the problem was to get Stickeen across. As Muir cut the steps in the ice and made his own way across, Stickeen cried and moaned. Muir tried to calm the dog as he would a frightened boy. But Stickeen kept howling. Muir adds: "When I gained the other side, he screamed louder than ever, and after running back and forth in vain search for a way of escape, he would return to the brink of the crevasse above the bridge, moaning and wailing as if in the bitterness of death. Could this be the silent, philosophic Stickeen? I shouted encouragement, telling him the bridge was not so bad as it looked, that I had left it flat and safe for his feet, and he could walk it easily. But he was afraid to try. Strange so small an animal should be capable of such big, wise fears. I called again and again in a re-assuring tone to come on and fear nothing; that he could come if he would only try. He would hush for a moment, look down again at the bridge, and shout his unshakable conviction that he could never, never come that way; then lie back in despair, as if howling, 'O-o-oh! what a place! No-o-o, I can never go-o-o down there!' His natural composure and courage had vanished utterly in a tumultuous storm of fear. Had the danger been less, his distress would have seemed ridiculous. But in this dismal, merciless abyss lay the shadow of death, and his heart-rending cries might well have called Heaven to his help. Perhaps they did. So hidden before, he was now transpar-ent, and one could see the workings of his heart and mind like the movements of a clock out of its case. His voice and gesture, hopes and fears, were so perfectly human that none could mistake them; while he seemed to understand every word of mine. I was troubled at the thought of having to leave him out all night, and of the danger of not finding him in the morning. It seemed impossible to get him to venture. To compel him to try through fear of being abandoned,

I started off as if leaving him to his fate, and disappeared back of a hummock; but this did no good; he only lay down and moaned in utter hopeless misery. So, after hiding a few minutes, I went back to the brink of the crevasse and in a severe tone of voice shouted across to him that now I must certainly leave him, I could wait no longer, and that, if he would not come, all I could promise was that I would return to seek him next day. I warned him that if he went back to the woods the wolves would kill him, and finished by urging him once more by words and gestures to come on, come on.

"He knew very well what I meant, and at last, with the courage of despair, hushed and breathless, he crouched down on the brink in the hollow I had made for my knees, pressed his body against the ice as if trying to get the advantage of the friction of every hair, gazed into the first step, put his little feet together and slid down slowly, slowly over the edge and down into it, bunching all four in it and almost standing on his head. Then, without lifting his feet, as well as I could see through the snow, he slowly worked them over the edge of the step and down into the next and the next in succession in the same way, and gained the end of the bridge. Then, lifting his feet with the regularity and slowness of the vibrations of a seconds pendulum, as if counting and measuring *one-two-three,* holding himself steady against the gusty wind, and giving separate attention to each little step, he gained the foot of the cliff, while I was on my knees leaning over to give him a lift should he succeed in getting within reach of my arm. Here he halted in dead silence, and it was here I feared he might fail, for dogs are poor climbers. I had no cord. If I had had one, I would have dropped a noose over his head and hauled him up. But while I was thinking whether an available cord might be made out of clothing, he was looking keenly into the series of notched steps and fingerholds I had made, as if counting them, and fixing the position of each one of them in his mind. Then suddenly up he came in a springy rush, hooking his paws into the steps and notches so quickly that I could not see how it was done, and whizzed past my head, safe at last!"

Muir tried to catch the dog and caress him. But Stickeen ran with joy that was uncontrolled. Muir wrote: "He flashed and darted hither and thither as if fairly demented, screaming and shouting, swirling round and round in giddy loops and circles like a leaf in a whirlwind, lying down, and rolling over and over, sidewise and heels over head, and pouring forth a tumultous flood of hysterical cries and sobs and gasping mutterings. When I ran up to shake him, fearing he might die of joy, he flashed off two or three hundred yards, his feet in a mist of motion; then, turning suddenly, came back in a wild rush and launched himself at my face, almost knocking me down, all the time screeching and screaming and shouting as if saying, 'Saved! saved! saved!' Then away again, dropping suddenly at times with his feet in the air, trembling and fairly sobbing."

Muir and the dog reached camp safely at ten o'clock. Stickeen was much too tired to eat. The little dog had nightmares that night and many nights later, doubtless dreaming that he was on the brink of a terrible crevasse too wide to jump. He was Muir's constant companion for the rest of their journey. At night he would put his head on Muir's knee and look at Muir as if he were trying to say, "Wasn't that an awful time we had together on the glacier?"

Muir learned much about glaciers on this trip with Stickeen. What he saw of the workings of these gigantic Alaskan icefields confirmed many of his theories about glaciation in the Sierra. Yet he learned more than this. He now knew how warm and joyous the friendship between a man and a dog can be. He learned that dogs as well as men can rise to heroic heights when danger threatens. He learned that a man and his dog, working as a team, can sometimes make a contribution to human knowledge.

A HOME AND A FORTUNE

IN AUGUST 1880, John Muir—then forty-two years old—married dark-haired Louie Wanda Strentzel, who, like his mother, understood him. She was twenty-seven years old and the daughter of a Pole, John Strentzel, and his wife, Louisiana. Mr. Strentzel had fled Poland in 1830 to escape the Russians, who had put down a revolution he had helped inspire. Eventually he settled near Martinez, California. Though he was trained as a physician, in California he became a farmer, having extensive holdings of land where he grew grapes, cherries, and other fruits. He gave some of the land to the young couple.

At the time of his marriage, Muir had saved several thousand dollars. He was by that time a noted magazine writer, known all over the country.

After his marriage, Muir became a fruit farmer. He cleared land and planted vineyards and orchards and in ten years made himself a fortune. There was no income tax in those days. Everything above expenses could be saved. During this period he put aside about $100,000. He thought that amount was enough to supply all the needs of his wife and two young daughters. Accordingly, he sold part of the Martinez property.

While he was farming, he and his wife agreed that between July and October of each year he was to be free for wilderness wandering. During those months there was a lull in the work. Soft fruits, such as cherries, had been harvested, and the rest would not be ripe until October. So it was that Muir went off on many expeditions in these summer months.

This does not suggest that he was not an earnest orchardist. He put in many fruit trees and vines, doing the work himself. He had a gift for making things grow—a "green thumb." And his orchards and vineyards did well. Dr. Strentzel had developed many varieties of fruit. Muir decided to concentrate on those fruits that brought the highest price in the market. These were Bartlett pears and Tokay grapes.

As a result of the excellent quality of his fruit, the merchants bid high, and Muir's profits mounted. He was a good trader and was seldom outdone on a deal. One time all the buyers, acting in unison, agreed to offer Muir a very low price. Muir refused, and that day no Muir fruit was sold. The next day Muir got twice the price he had been offered the day before.

He took his money to the banks in Martinez in a laundry bag, driving a horse and buggy. He was tall, lean, brown-bearded, and known to all the people of that area. He was an able businessman

and fruit grower. He could have continued to make more and more money. But he was unhappy on the farm.

During this period of farming, the Muirs had two daughters. As soon as they could talk, John taught them the names of all the flowers that bloomed near the ranch. He tried to pass on to them his love of the wilderness. He thought that the best classroom was "Nature's school—the one true University." He earnestly felt that children should know the names of plants and animals around them. "How would you like it," he asked his daughter Wanda, "if people didn't call you by your name?"

Also during this period, John went East to see his father, who was dying. John forgave his father for the cruelty he had shown to him when he was a boy, and his father was sorry for the way he had once treated John. It came about in this way. John had a sister Joanna born in Wisconsin, and Joanna later had a baby girl, Ethel. John's father went to live with Joanna and her husband in Missouri and grew very fond of little Ethel. The love and tenderness he had not given John he gave to Ethel. People said that Ethel taught John's father that love is more powerful than cruelty. Through Ethel, John's father came to realize how wrong he had been in his treatment of John as a boy.

John was at his father's bedside when he died. Though he was very old and very ill, he recognized his son, saying, "Is this my dear John?" Then he took John by the hand and drew him down to kiss him, and he held his hand for a long time, not wanting John to leave.

"My dear wanderer, my dear wanderer," his father said when speaking of John. And when his father died, John wept.

John returned to his farm in California. But the green meadows, the cool streams, and the high peaks of the mountains kept calling him. He had tilled the soil in Wisconsin and knew the drudgery of it. When he was farming in California he felt like a wild animal in a cage. His longing for the mountains was so strong that the dull, monotonous work made him ill. His wife was understanding and knew that he was made for the mountains, not for the farm. So she planned to get rid of most of the property, selling off some land and leasing other portions. Under her guidance this was done, and by the tenth year John was through with farming and back in the woods he loved — hiking and camping, and then returning to civilization to tell people through his lectures, his drawings, and his writings what the wilderness means to humankind.

The wilderness, in John Muir's eyes, was a place where worn-out people could get well, where nervous people could become strong. The wilderness has beauty and harmony. There is music in flowing water. Wind in the trees is soothing. The songs of birds, the chattering of squirrels, the call of loons, the flights of ducks all remind us that we are only one of many forms of life on this planet. The other animals — and the flowers too — are our companions. They are part of the universal scheme that keeps the earth a place of beauty and wonder. Clean rivers, hillsides that have not been eroded, thick woods, the songs of birds, the fragrance of forests —

these are God's creations that humankind must help preserve. This was the message John Muir wanted to carry to the people of America. That is why he left the farm behind and turned once more to the mountains — so that he could write and talk and tell the people of the great glories of the mountains and meadows that must be preserved.

MOUNTAIN
CLIMBING

MUIR TRAVELED incessantly for days and weeks on end in the Sierra, going by foot and collecting with care all the data he needed to educate people on the values of the wilderness. Most people going for a hike or a climb take hours or even days to prepare for the event. But John Muir, people said, merely jumped over the back fence and was on his way. He did, indeed, take hardly any time to get ready, carrying little more than a change of underwear and socks and a few toilet articles. A blanket tied in a roll was his bed. His food was usually only bread carried in a sack. He had tea, a cup, a small kettle, matches, and a knife for whittling kindling. An ice axe was essential for the ascent of snowfields and glaciers, and he used hobnails on the soles of his shoes to keep from slipping. He depended on campfires to keep him warm. Muir knew where to find the pitch pine that makes a quick hot fire even in wet weather. And he often kept his fire going all night, so that he needed only one blanket. In case of rain or snow, he would find a cave in a cliff or look for a log that was big enough to serve as a roof over his head.

Muir hiked over practically all of the Sierra while making his studies of glaciers and collecting materials for his books. He came to know these mountains in rain and sunshine, in all the seasons of the year, when the bloom of the flowers was at its peak and when the winds howled, bringing hail and snow. Muir, who was always thin and wiry, traveled for days on end with nothing but bread and tea for meals. His legs were strong; his wind was excellent. He went up mountains like a sheep or goat. But he early learned that mountain climbing can be dangerous.

Once while climbing Mount Watkins (8235 feet) he was walking across the top of a thousand-foot cliff when he slipped and fell backward, striking his head and losing consciousness. He would have been killed had he not been caught by bushes. When he regained consciousness, he was "trembling as if cold, not injured in the slightest." Muir made these comments about the accident: "Judging by the sun, I could not have been insensible very long; probably not a minute, possibly an hour; and I could not remember what made me fall, or where I had fallen from; but I saw that if I had rolled a little further, my mountain-climbing would have been finished, for just beyond the bushes the cañon wall steepened and I might have fallen to the bottom. 'There,' said I, addressing my feet, to whose separate skill I had learned to trust night and day on any mountain, 'that is what you get by intercourse with stupid town stairs, and dead pavements.' I felt degraded and worthless. I had not yet reached the most difficult portion of the cañon, but I determined to guide my humbled body over the most nerve-trying places I could find; for I was now awake, and felt confident that the last of the town fog had been shaken from both head and feet."

Muir was the first to climb Mount Ritter (13,156 feet), where he scaled a very dangerous cliff alone, without the help of ropes. He had ascended about 12,800 feet when he reached a sheer cliff. He tried to scale it and he had a moment of fright and terror that most alpinists know: "After gaining a point about halfway to the top, I was suddenly brought to a dead stop, with arms outspread, clinging close to the face of the rock, unable to move hand or foot either up or down. My doom appeared fixed. I *must* fall. There would be a moment of bewilderment, and then a lifeless rumble down the one general precipice to the glacier below.

"When this final danger flashed upon me, I became nerve-shaken for the first time since setting foot on the mountains, and my mind seemed to fill with a stifling smoke. But this terrible eclipse lasted only a moment, when life blazed forth again with preternatural clearness. I seemed suddenly to become possessed of a new sense. The other self, bygone experiences, Instinct, or Guardian Angel,—call it what you will,—came forward and assumed control. Then my trembling muscles became firm again, every rift and flaw in the rock was seen as through a microscope, and my limbs moved with a positiveness and precision with which I seemed to have nothing at all to do. Had I been borne aloft upon wings, my deliverance could not have been more complete."

Muir went north to the State of Washington and climbed Mount Rainier (14,408 feet) one day when he was not feeling well. Even so, the ascent was to him a lark. Yet expert climbers consider Mount Rainier a difficult ascent. The same is true of Mount Whitney (14,495 feet), the highest of our mountains south of Alaska. Muir climbed this high peak of the Sierra alone. He was indeed the first one to find a way to the top from the east. Yet it was on Mount Shasta (14,161 feet) that he had his most dangerous experience.

This climb of Shasta was in November. The snow was thick even at the base of the mountain. Muir slept only an hour and a half that night and started climbing at about 2:00 A.M. He was in snow up to his knees all the way up, and it was so deep he sometimes sank to his armpits. He had 10,000 feet to climb from his camp to the summit; the cold was intense; and the dry, shifting snow filled the air with a dust that made breathing difficult. Even so, he made the top in eight and a half hours. A storm was coming up as he left the peak, but he reached the base before it broke. He scooped out a shelter behind some lava rocks where the wind did not reach him and made his bed there. The storm came that night, piling huge drifts of snow over his shelter. He had a good supply of wood to keep a fire going and stayed there five days while the storm wore itself out.

This snowstorm filled him with excitement. He had a magnifying glass through which he examined the snow crystals, as he lay

for hours watching the snow being driven by the wind and the dwarf pine trees bowing in the gale. Before the five days were over, he had company. A squirrel came to visit him, and a few mountain sheep sought shelter behind some of the dwarf pines just above his shelter. People in the valley were sure that Muir had perished in this storm and sent a search party looking for him. But Muir, who knew the mountains well, knew how to take care of himself in storms as well as sunshine.

One time, however, he almost perished on Shasta. Late in April he had taken a party to the top, and, after resting one day, went up again with a companion to make some weather observations. The two of them ascended swiftly and made their observations at nine o'clock and again at one o'clock. By this time it was obvious that a severe storm was coming. The men knew it was wise to leave the mountain top at once, but Muir wanted to make his three o'clock reading, so they stayed. By three o'clock the storm had broken in full fury. First came hail, then snow. The temperature dropped twenty-two degrees in a few minutes and then went below zero. The wind was now a gale; the dark clouds produced blackness like night. Lightning flashed again and again, and thunder was loud and continuous. The first mile and a half down the mountain was along a narrow ridge flanked by steep cliffs. It was extremely dangerous walking in the darkness of this cold, furious storm. So the men decided to stay on the mountain.

Shortly below the top are hot springs where steam bubbles up through mud. The men sought shelter there. There was no cave in which to hide. The only way they could keep from freezing to death or dying from exposure was to lie flat in the warm mud on their backs. The escaping steam was so hot there was always the danger of scalding, so while they lay in the mud they had to keep squirming to keep from being burned. The greater danger was from the escaping gases. John Muir knew, from his boyhood experience in digging the well, how dangerous carbonic gas can be. This steam that came spurting through the mud was partly carbonic acid. John warned his companion of it and made certain that they spoke to each other frequently, making sure the other was alive. They had to fight off sleep, for one who slumbered might easily be killed by the carbonic acid that gathered when the wind died down.

For thirteen hours they lay on their backs in this hot mud. Their undersides, in the mud, were almost scorched; but their topsides, exposed to the elements, were chilled. Snow had covered them and then melted and frozen into ice. Their clothes were frozen. The storm finally stopped and dawn came. They were so weak they could hardly stand, and their trousers were so thick with ice they could scarcely bend them at the knee. But they staggered down the mountain to safety. Five thousand feet below the summit only three inches of snow had fallen, and at the base of Mount Shasta there had been only a light rain. The storm — though fierce and dangerous — had been confined to the top of the mountain. In spite of his strength and powers of endurance, Muir was so weak when he got off the mountain that he could not walk. He had to be helped onto a horse, and he was in bed for several days.

While the two men saved their lives, they came off the mountain with frozen feet—one of the most painful of all injuries. To save their feet, they had to thaw them out very, very slowly. This meant keeping them in snow for several hours. Other climbers, who have not been so careful, have lost some or all of their toes and fingers. Though Muir did not lose any toes from this freezing, his feet caused him some trouble ever afterwards.

Muir climbed hundreds of peaks but left very few accounts of the ascents. He was a good alpinist; however, the techniques and tribulations of mountain climbing were not of great concern to him. What he enjoyed most were the views from the tops of the peaks he scaled. From these heights he saw many of the glories of the universe. On these peaks he felt close to God. There he gained inspiration for the lectures he gave and the books he wrote. These climbs were one way to slough off cares and worries and come to know the great glories of the outdoors.

THE MUSIC OF
THE TREES

THE TREES of the Sierra were John Muir's great love. He saw lumber interests cutting them in reckless ways. People sometimes set fires to forests on purpose, hoping that grass would grow for their sheep. Civilization, so called, was making ruinous invasions into the wilderness. So John Muir became an eloquent and powerful advocate who maintained that some forests should be preserved in their wilderness state, and that any forest that was cut for timber should never be mutilated or destroyed.

He had a special love for the dwarf pine that grows on the high ridges. There it is only a foot or two high, for the low temperatures and cold, cutting winds prevent it from reaching up. So it reaches out, hugging the ground and getting warmth from the rocks. Muir greatly admired this pine. It thrives under severe conditions; it is in most respects the sturdiest of all the trees. Muir examined the rings on the trunks of these pines and found some were 400 years old. But in spite of their age, their trunks were only six inches in diameter. These dwarf pines have supple branches that one can tie in knots. And they grow so low and so thick on the high ridges that they are good hiding places. Muir often slept under them, as do the deer and mountain sheep. This pine and the juniper, Muir said, "are never blown down, so long as they continue in good health."

He saw storms in the Sierra that did great destruction. "But when the storm is over, and we behold the same forests tranquil again, towering fresh and unscathed in erect majesty, and consider what centuries of storms have fallen upon them since they were first planted—hail, to break the tender seedlings; lightning, to scorch and shatter; snow, winds, and avalanches, to crush and over-whelm—while the manifest result of all this wild storm-culture is the glorious perfection we behold; then faith in Nature's forestry is established, and we cease to deplore the violence of her most de-structive gales, or of any other storm-implement whatsoever."

Muir liked the way the trees behaved in windstorms. They bowed like willows in a gale. And their needles vibrated so fast in a high wind that they made a distinct hum. Muir called it "the finest music" the wind produces in the Sierra.

Once when a great windstorm came up, he went into the woods to see the storm in all its fury and beauty. "I heard trees falling for hours at the rate of one every two or three minutes; some uprooted, partly on account of the loose, water-soaked condition of the ground; others broken straight across, where some weakness caused by fire had determined the spot. The gestures of the various trees made a delightful study. The force of the gale was such that the most steadfast monarch of them all rocked down to its roots with a motion plainly perceptible when one leaned against it. Nature was holding high festival, and every fiber of the most rigid giants thrilled with glad excitement.

"I drifted on through the midst of this passionate music and motion, across many a glen, from ridge to ridge; often halting in the lee of a rock for shelter, or to gaze and listen. Even when the grand anthem had swelled to its highest pitch, I could distinctly hear the varying tones of individual trees — Spruce, and Fir, and Pine, and leafless Oak — and even the infinitely gentle rustle of the withered grasses at my feet. Each was expressing itself in its own way — singing its own peculiar gestures — manifesting a richness of variety to be found in no other forest I have yet seen."

Muir climbed a hundred-foot pine tree in the windstorm and stayed in its top for several hours. The wind was so strong that the treetop swung in an arc of twenty to thirty degrees. He learned from this experience that each pine needle has a separate tone. The needles click on each other, making a distinct note, and needles that do not strike one another hum in the high wind.

Probably Muir's choicest friend whom he met on his hikes through the forests of the Sierra was the Douglas squirrel. It is related to the eastern red squirrel but smaller in size. After many hours watching him, Muir wrote: "He is, without exception, the

wildest animal I ever saw — a fiery, sputtering little bolt of life, lux-uriating in quick oxygen and the woods' best juices. One can hardly think of such a creature being dependent, like the rest of us, on climate and food. But, after all, it requires no long acquaintance to learn he is human, for he works for a living. His busiest time is in the Indian summer. Then he gathers burs and hazel-nuts like a plodding farmer, working continuously every day for hours; saying not a word; cutting off the ripe cones at the top of his speed, as if employed by the job, and examining every branch in regular order, as if careful that not one should escape him; then, descending, he stores them away beneath logs and stumps, in anticipation of the pinching hunger days of winter."

On almost every trip in spring, summer, or fall Muir made some mention of this fine animal. He said in words of high praise: "How long the life of a Douglas Squirrel may be, I don't know. The young seem to sprout from knot-holes, perfect from the first, and as enduring as their own trees. It is difficult, indeed, to realize that so condensed a piece of sun-fire should ever become dim or die at all. He is seldom killed by hunters, for he is too small to encourage much of their attention. In the lower and middle zones a few fall a prey to rattlesnakes. Occasionally he is pursued by hawks and wild-cats, etc. But, upon the whole, he dwells safely in the deep bosom of the woods, the most highly favored of all his happy tribe. May his tribe increase!"

Muir spent many days measuring and studying the Big Trees (*Sequoiadendron gigantea*) of the Sierra. There are two kinds of sequoia in California. One species, found in the Coast Ranges, is *Sequoia sempervirens*. Today it is called the "coast redwood." These trees are the highest in the world, some rising over 360 feet. They are in such thick groves that very little direct sunshine reaches the ground. Some people like these groves best of all.

Muir, however, liked the *Sequoiadendron gigantea* best. Found in the Sierra, it is often called the "Sierra redwood." It does not grow in thick groves. The trees stand farther apart, and sunshine lightens up the forest around them. The tops are normally pointed like a cone, unless storms have broken them off. The more Muir saw of these giants, the more impressed he was. Up, up, up they rose above all other trees. "Columns of sunshine," Muir called them. They were so massive, so overwhelming, he called them "King." "Do behold the King in his glory, King Sequoia," he wrote a friend. This tree was also to be important in his life. One of his great deeds in later years was to help preserve its groves from destruction.

He found Big Trees over thirty-five feet in diameter and he walked softly and reverently among them. He estimated that one sequoia was more than 4000 years old. Muir described this tree, which he found on a journey into the Kings River canyon: "The largest, and as far as I know the oldest, of all the King's River trees that I saw is the majestic stump, about a hundred and forty feet high, which above the swell of the roots is thirty-five feet and eight inches inside the bark, and over four thousand years old. It was burned nearly half through at the base, and I spent a day in chopping off the charred surface, cutting into the heart, and counting the wood-rings with the aid of a lens. I made out a little over four thousand without difficulty or doubt, but I was unable to get a complete count, owing to confusion in the rings where wounds had been healed over. Judging by what is left of it, this was a fine, tall, symmetrical tree nearly forty feet in diameter before it lost its bark."

Thanks to Muir, there are hundreds of sequoias standing today. The Big Trees that Muir greatly admired are preserved in Sequoia National Park and Yosemite National Park and in the Calaveras Big Trees State Park managed by the State of California. There are also stands of Big Trees in federal forests in California, and the policy of the Forest Service is not to log them.

The largest of the Big Trees is known as General Sherman. Located in what is now Kings Canyon National Park, the tree is 272 feet high and about 37 feet in diameter at its base. If it were tunneled, three cars could drive through it abreast, for its trunk is as wide as a city street. It is almost 3500 years old and has about 2000 tons of wood in it—enough to build forty five-room houses.

On one of his excursions into the sequoia forests, Muir found a hermit living in a remote log cabin. Muir relates how this man, too, was interested in the Big Trees: "One of the greatest of his trees stands a little way back of his cabin, and he proudly led me to it, bidding me admire its colossal proportions and measure it to see if in all the forest there could be another so grand. It proved to be only twenty-six feet in diameter, and he seemed distressed to learn that the Mariposa Grizzly Giant was larger. I tried to comfort him by observing that his was the taller, finer formed, and perhaps the more favorably situated."

The bark of these Big Trees is sometimes two feet thick, and their seeds are so light that it takes 3000 of them to make one ounce. The coast redwoods often sprout from old roots or stumps, but the Big Tree in the Sierra grows only from seeds. Only a few of the seeds are fertile, and they need sunshine, good soil, and moisture to grow. Thanks again to Muir, there are thousands of tiny trees in the Sierra that will be giants in their own right a few thousand years from now.

Muir learned how fire damages the forests. A fire among pines not only races along the ground but often runs up the tree trunks and then jumps from treetop to treetop, going as fast as a horse can run. This is called a "crown fire"—the most dangerous in the woods. But a sequoia fire is different. The ground fire creeps slowly among them. When the forest is really dry, the flames run up the furrows in the bark of the trees. The Big Tree contains tannic acid, a chemical used in some fire extinguishers. So when the bark gets thick, it protects the trunk. It takes indeed a furious fire to kill a Big Tree, even though, when the flames reach the top, they burst forth in a blaze. Muir saw these fires at night. Logs on the forest floor were covered with flames, giving off a ruby glow. Fire streamers ran up the trunks. The treetops were like big lamps. The flames were so bright that Muir could read a book at a distance of 300 yards.

Muir discovered that some fires were set by sheepherders who thought that burning made land more fertile and that it would produce better grazing the next year. These fires burned down large forests of pine and fir and of younger sequoias that had not yet developed a thick bark.

Muir was particularly worried about the way the lumber mills were destroying the Big Trees. They were so large that they were difficult to chop or saw down. So lumbermen often dynamited them. This caused waste and destruction of much valuable wood. Muir feared that if these practices continued and if the forests were not protected, they would soon be gone. He therefore set out to protect the forests from destruction.

PUBLIC SERVICE

JOHN MUIR never held public office, but his public service was of a high order. As early as 1870 he realized that preservation of the American wilderness was necessary for all the people.

First was the need for forests and alpine meadows to ensure a water supply. Without the forests to protect the slopes from quick runoffs and to store the water underground, and without the high meadows to act as reservoirs, the lowlands would become deserts in some parts of the country. That was particularly true of the West, where farmers were dependent on irrigation.

Second was the need for forests and high meadows for recreation and pleasure. Over and over again Muir said, "Everybody needs beauty as well as bread, places to play in and pray in, where Nature may heal and cheer and give strength to body and soul alike."

Muir knew people's hunger for the wilderness. He would come back from his hikes out of San Francisco with his arms full of flowers, and the children, who had only streets for playgrounds, would beg him for some.

Muir had also seen people in dark apartments in San Francisco cultivating flowers and other plants in tin cans, buckets, and dishes. They were, Muir said, "humble plant friends" of these poor people.

Muir knew from his own experiences that life in the woods was healthy. He knew that living in the woods made some sick people well. He knew that it was good for men and women to escape the noise and smoke and dirt of the cities and get into the great cathedrals of the mountains.

Muir had also seen with his own eyes the result of overgrazing by sheep and cattle. In the early 1870s he estimated that the grass and seedling trees of nine-tenths of the Sierra had been eaten down so close as to make the whole range look like the inside of a dusty corral. He saw trees being cut everywhere in wholesale fashion. The forests were being destroyed. The dynamiting of the Big Trees caused losses so great that only about a third of each tree was saved for timber. He saw forests burning with no one to control the fires. He saw the result of these practices in the valleys as well as in the mountains. The streams were now dark with mud and silt. The rain and snow water, no longer held in the mountains by roots of grass and plants, was running off the slopes and washing countless tons of dirt down into the rivers.

He saw that the property rights in the waters of the rivers and lakes of the mountains had been acquired by private operators, speculators, and corporations who were using all the water for themselves or selling it at very high prices. Many farmers who could not afford to pay high prices for water left their farms or sold them to the big operators. Those who had not been starved out began to organize groups to defend their rights.

The waters of lakes and streams, the forests on high ridges, the woods in deep valleys, alpine meadows, grass, flowers, shrubs — these belonged to all the people, not to a select group. If the earth was not to be ruined for the benefit of the few, the people must be organized. So Muir decided to dedicate the rest of his life to that end. He became the spokesman of the people. His aim was to protect some sections of the forests in parks or preserves where no cutting could ever take place. In 1864 Congress had passed an act that President Lincoln approved, granting some of the Yosemite to California for a state park. A large gorge was included and valley land that was fifteen miles long and two miles wide. Four sections of groves of the Big Sequoia were also transferred to California. In 1872 Congress created Yellowstone National Park. But Muir was convinced more parks were needed.

Muir also wanted to restrict or control grazing by sheep and cattle so that the high ridges and meadows would not, as a consequence of overgrazing, be eroded by rain. He decided to educate the people of America on the values of the great wilderness areas in California and in other states and to arouse them to action.

By 1889 Muir had put all other work behind him and gave most of his time to the cause of conservation.

Robert Underwood Johnson, an editor of *Century* magazine

from the East, went with Muir into the Sierra and saw the havoc and ruin in the forests. The two men believed that California alone could not properly protect this wonderful land from destructive logging and uncontrolled grazing. They decided to work together to make Yosemite a *national* park and keep all grazing and lumbering operations out of it for all time. They got a bill introduced in Congress but it failed to pass that year.

Muir wrote articles for Johnson's magazine and for newspapers. These articles whipped up public sentiment for conservation. And on October 1, 1890, Yosemite National Park was created by a bill signed by President Harrison. A cavalry patrol from the United States Army was sent to the area to guard the new park property.

At about the same time, two additional national parks were created in California to save the sequoia trees. One was Sequoia National Park and the other was General Grant National Park, which is now part of Kings Canyon National Park.

In 1892 Muir helped organize the Sierra Club. It had as one of its objectives the preservation of the forests and other natural features of the Sierra Nevada. Muir was the Club's first president and held that office until his death.

One of Muir's closest workers and advisers in the Sierra Club was William E. Colby, who shared most of Muir's victories and defeats. "Blood, sweat, and tears" is the way Muir and Colby won their battles to save the forests and meadows. Through the Sierra Club, conservationists presented a united front. The club, with Muir, was responsible for getting forest lands set aside either as national forests or as national parks.

The sentiment that Muir and the Sierra Club had created for saving public lands was now having great effect. By 1893 the federal government had set aside 13 million more acres as forest reserves, and while it did not yet have an organized staff to keep all the trespassing sheepherders and lumbermen out, much of the public lands were saved from destruction.

A commission of six men was appointed by the government to survey other parts of the country to see if there were more forests that should be saved from destruction. Muir worked with the commission and helped them make their survey. They found the Black Hills in South Dakota being ruined. Portions of the Big Horn Mountains in Wyoming had been reduced to a forest of stumps. In Idaho and Montana they found misuse of forest lands. They found the same conditions in Oregon and Washington. They found other areas in California that were being ruined by sheep and by lumber operations.

The commision made its report in 1897, recommending two new national parks—Grand Canyon and Mount Rainier—and urging that thirteen national forests be created in eight western states. President Cleveland set aside the lands for the thirteen national forests.

This action by Cleveland made the lumber, sheep, cattle, and mining industries furious. Their lobbyists moved into Washington,

D.C., and Congress was persuaded to suspend Cleveland's order. The Department of Interior opened the forest reserves to private claims. Hundreds of private claims were filed.

Muir wrote in reply: "Even in Congress a sizable chunk of gold, carefully concealed, will outtalk and outfight all the nation on a subject like forestry, well smothered in ignorance, and in which the money interests of only a few are conspicuously involved. Under these circumstances, the bawling, blethering oratorical stuff drowns the voice of God himself."

Muir went on to plead with the people, whose votes ultimately count, to save their inheritance of the forests from destruction. He ended one stirring article with these words: "Any fool can destroy trees. They cannot run away; and if they could, they would still be destroyed—chased and hunted down as long as fun or a dollar could be got out of their bark hides, branching horns, or magnificent bole backbones. Few that fell trees plant them; nor would planting avail much towards getting back anything like the noble primeval forests. It took more than three thousand years to make some of the trees in these Western woods—trees that are still standing in perfect strength and beauty, waving and singing in the mighty forests of the Sierra. Through all the wonderful, eventful centuries God has cared for these trees, saved them from drought, disease, avalanches, and a thousand straining, leveling tempests and floods; but he cannot save them from fools—only Uncle Sam can do that."

Muir wrote many other articles, and eventually the sentiment in Congress changed. Theodore Roosevelt became President. Muir and many others urged him to create a Bureau of Forestry to manage the forest reserves. Roosevelt persuaded Congress to do that.

In May 1903, Roosevelt came to Yosemite to have Muir show him the valley and its forests. They camped one night under the Big Trees; they rode horses high above the Yosemite floor and camped out two more nights. From Glacier Point Muir pointed out the great peaks and valleys to Roosevelt and told him how important these forests and water resources were to all the people. Muir told Roosevelt about "the timber thieves, and the destructive work of the lumbermen, and other spoilers of the forests." Muir convinced Roosevelt that vigorous action was necessary if these natural resources all over America were to be saved for all the people.

Roosevelt described this trip with Muir in glowing terms: "Lying out at night under those giant sequoias was lying in a temple built by no hand of man, a temple grander than any human architect could by any possibility build, and I hope for the preservation of the groves of giant trees simply because it would be a shame to our civilization to let them disappear. They are monuments in themselves."

Not all of the Yosemite country was in the national park that had been created in 1890. The State of California still owned Yosemite Valley itself. In 1904 Muir helped a campaign get under way to

have California cede back to the United States this important land that Congress had granted California in 1864. After a great struggle, the bill was passed by the California legislature. But the question remained whether Congress would accept the gift. Lumber interests moved into Washington, D.C., saying they wanted the sugar pine trees for cutting. Other private interests wanted part of the land for water reservoirs, grazing, and other purposes. Muir and the Sierra Club worked hard to get the bill through Congress. At last they succeeded, and in 1906 Yosemite Valley became part of the national park.

A demand arose to turn a portion of the park into a water reservoir for San Francisco. This was known as the Hetch Hetchy project, from the name of the valley. Muir and the Sierra Club opposed this move. There were other water supplies available outside the park. After President Roosevelt had visited Yosemite with Muir, he encouraged Muir in trying to save Hetch Hetchy. Muir threw himself into the fight. He wrote: "A great political miracle, this of 'improving' the beauty of the most beautiful of all mountain parks by cutting down its groves, and burying all the thickets of azalea and wild rose, lily gardens, and ferneries two or three hundred feet deep. After this is done we are promised a road blasted on the slope of the north wall, where nature-lovers may sit on rustic stools, or rocks, like frogs on logs, to admire the sham dam lake, the grave of Hetch Hetchy. This Yosemite Park fight began a dozen years ago.

Never for a moment have I believed that the American people would fail to defend it for the welfare of themselves and all the world. The people are now aroused. Tidings from far and near show that almost every good man and woman is with us. Therefore be of good cheer, watch, and pray and fight!"

When Taft became President he also visited Yosemite, and he and Muir walked the four miles from Glacier Point to the floor of the valley. Muir convicced Taft that the beautiful Hetch Hetchy Valley should not be turned into a reservoir.

Muir loved Hetch Hetchy. Its beauties had not yet been marred by axe and plow, sheep and cattle. He saw other parts of the Sierra being trampled into dust and made a desert. He wanted to save Hetch Hetchy both from that fate and from the even more awful fate of being submerged forever under the waters of a reservoir.

But Muir lost the fight. President Wilson, inaugurated in 1913, named Franklin K. Lane as Secretary of the Interior. Lane was from San Francisco and an ardent advocate of the Hetch Hetchy project. He had been city attorney for San Francisco and had filed that city's application for the project. So the Hetch Hetchy reservoir was later authorized by Congress and Muir was defeated.

This defeat hastened Muir's death. He died of pneumonia in Los Angeles on Christmas Eve, 1914. Only some two years after his death was a law enacted that placed all the national parks under one director who was empowered to "conserve the scenery and the natural and historic objects and the wild life" in the parks. This had been one of Muir's projects, and the men who took charge of the parks in 1916 carried out Muir's ideas. So in a true sense Muir was the father of our national parks.

Muir wrote near the end of his life: "In the beginning of my studies I never intended to write a word for the press. In my life of lonely wanderings I was pushed and pulled, on and on, through everything, by unwavering never-ending love of God's earth plans and works, and eternal, immortal, all-embracing Beauty."

Muir loved the trees that stood as sentinels on the edges of alpine basins, the Douglas squirrel and the water ouzel, the waterfalls, the clear rushing creeks, the sapphire lakes lying above glacial moraines, the thickly matted meadows where roots of grass and plants hold water back and fashion reservoirs in the mountains better than any that people can build. A person in pursuit of gain can be a destructive force. A person in pursuit of beauty will find cathedrals in the woods and mountain gorges where his or her heart will be filled with wonder.

Knowing of people's love of beauty and their great need for it, Muir gave his life to help them discover beauty in the earth around them and to arouse their desire to protect it. The machine, Muir knew, could easily level the woods and make the land desolate. Humankind's mission on earth is not to destroy: it is to protect and conserve all living things. There is a place for trees and flowers and birds, as well as for people. Never should we try to crowd them out of the universe.

Humankind is but one form of life on this planet. We must learn to cherish and protect all other forms. They lift our hearts and are indispensable to our welfare. These are the messages John Muir carried to the American people. Though he lost some battles, Muir, more than any other person, made conservation a powerful, positive force in our national life.

INDEX